The Contemplative Face of
Old Testament Wisdom

The Contemplative Face
of Old Testament
Wisdom

in the context of world religions

JOHN EATON

SCM PRESS
London

TRINITY PRESS INTERNATIONAL
Philadelphia

First published 1989

SCM Press
26–30 Tottenham Road
London N1 4BZ

Trinity Press International
3725 Chestnut Street
Philadelphia, Pa. 19104

British Library Cataloguing in Publication Data

Eaton, J. H. (John Herbert, 1927–)
 The contemplative face of Old Testament Wisdom in the
 context of world religions.
 1. Bible. O.T. Wisdom literature. Critical studies
 I. Title
 223'.06

 ISBN 0–334–01913–3

Library of Congress Cataloging-in-Publication Data

Eaton, John (John H.)
 The contemplative face of Old Testament wisdom: in the context of
 world religions / John Eaton.
    p.   cm.
 Includes bibliographical references.
 ISBN 0–334–01913–3
 1. Wisdom literature—Criticism, interpretation, etc. 2. Bible.
O.T. Hagiographa—Criticism, interpretation, etc. 3. Wisdom–
–Religious aspects—Comparative studies. 4. Contemplation–
–Comparative studies. I. Title.
BS1455.E27 1989
223'.06—dc20   89–37673

Typeset at The Spartan Press Ltd, Lymington, Hampshire
and printed in Great Britain by
The Camelot Press Ltd, Southampton

For dearest Margaret

Mighty waters cannot put out the light of love
nor rivers overwhelm it.

Song of Songs 8.7

Contents

Preface

After a period of relative neglect, the Old Testament wisdom books are gaining more attention. There is a growing awareness that they may have particular value for the spiritual quest of our time. As a contribution to this rediscovery the present study, after an introduction to the sources, sets out themes from five wisdom books (Proverbs, Job, Ecclesiastes, Ecclesiasticus, Sayings of the Fathers) along with material from the world's contemplative teachers. I hope in this way to make the contemplative aspect of Old Testament wisdom more recognizable.

This thematic treatment is followed by an exploration of 'wisdom psalms', where similar spiritual currents appear, though joining now with piety of sanctuary or scripture. Our encounter with all these beautiful texts, including eventually the Song of Songs, concludes with the direct question: what counsel does this wisdom offer the people of today?

To scholars and students I hope the study will be of value in showing the spiritual aspect of this Hebrew tradition in a coherent manner. For the general reader I hope there will be joy in meeting the gurus in these great texts and in profiting from their knowledge of reality and from their counsel.

Biblical texts are cited in my own translations. Translators of other texts are acknowledged gratefully in the notes. Where I have combined translations or made stylistic changes I have indicated the chief source by the phrase 'after so-and-so'.

I thank four friends from India for inspiration as I was writing: Aaloka and Sehdev Kumar (who introduced me to Kabir), and Mary and Solomon Raj (whose art crosses the cultures). My wife Margaret, with her knowledge of contemplative literature, has opened many doors and helped beyond words.

John Eaton

1

MEETING THE SOURCES

The noble roll

The rival claims of the world's religions can seem to discredit them all. Even a single religion soon divides into streams with contesting claims to truth. Well-informed people may be tempted to wash their hands of all of them.

But there is a remarkable witness to the reality with which the diverse religions engage. It is the voice of the contemplatives – consistent, though using the idioms of various ages and cultures. These are people who have dedicated themselves to watching and listening for the One, whom they refer to with such words as the Truth, the Way, the All, God. By paths of discipline, purity, humility, wonder and love, they approach their goal of union or communion with this One.

Beneath their differences of angle and emphasis the contemplatives of the world have a recognizably common love and commitment. We can pass through the records of them, from east to west, from ancient times to the present, without a break in the thread. From many periods and places we can draw up a noble roll of contemplatives, those who have taken a costly way to the final simplicity, the heart of all love. For them all the Indian poet Kabir might sing:

> I shall make
> My body into
> A clay lamp,
> My soul its wick,
> And my blood
> Oil!

Ah, the light
Of this lamp
Would reveal
The face
Of my Beloved
To me![1]

Can we include the Old Testament?

At first it might seem that of all religious classics the Old
Testament is least suited to be included in the noble roll. Is it
not a strident voice disturbing the harmony?

It is true that parts of this Hebrew Bible present a 'jealous'
God, fiercely hostile to other gods and alien forms of worship,
giving victory to one favoured people. It is true also that great
stress is laid here on the difference between God and human
beings, the holy Creator and the mere creature of dust – what
hope of union here? But these are strands in a larger pattern.
When all is considered, it appears that the Old Testament has
a great deal to contribute to the contemplative witness. This
accords with the fact that so many contemplatives are found
among the heirs of the Old Testament tradition: Jews,
Christians and Muslims.

When all is considered – yes, here is the challenge now
before us. All that we shall do can be but a beginning. Hearing
the voices of the Old Testament in a setting of the world's
contemplatives, we may hope to hear the Hebrew scriptures
in a fresh and rewarding manner and discover their contribution to the witness of the noble roll.

Wisdom and philosophy

Philosophy, the love of wisdom, has taken many forms and
directions. In our day it sometimes appears as a strictly
intellectual exercise, analysing the foundations of knowledge
and the uses of language. In earlier times, however, it was
often linked with the contemplative way. For Chinese,
Indians, Greeks and Jews, the philosopher, sage, or wise
person was likely to be one who attained wisdom through
contemplation. Our present consideration of the Old Testa-

ment, therefore, can well be founded on an appreciation of its philosophical books, the 'wisdom books': Proverbs, Job, Ecclesiastes and, as later witnesses to the tradition, Ecclesiasticus and the Sayings of the Fathers. We shall also refer to the Wisdom of Solomon and, near the end, discuss the beautiful Song of Songs. Psalms related to the wisdom books will also offer us valuable insights.

In modern times the wisdom books have often been undervalued. Theologians have passed them over rather quickly as offering little for a systematic theology of sin, grace and redemption. Philosophers have found here nothing akin to modern philosophy. The moral teachings were treated as mere advice for a prosperous life. The religious sentiments were regarded as only an after-thought of later compilers.

Recently the approaches have become more sympathetic.[2] It has begun to appear that the Hebrew tradition of wisdom, in all its main forms, is the fruit of a kind of contemplation. Its merits, then, would naturally elude a hasty, aggressive approach. Its statements need deep consideration, one by one. And it should prove a great help if we set beside it, theme by theme, materials from the world's contemplative literature. The Hebrew wisdom must indeed be interpreted in its own sense and contexts, but the comparisons should sharpen our senses to its depths and delights.

In preparation for this pleasant journey of comparison, here are some introductory remarks on our main sources.

The Book of Proverbs

The basic tradition of Hebrew wisdom is seen best in Proverbs. There are seven main collections of poetic teachings in the book, each section having its own heading. King Solomon is named in three of the headings, and in others the names of King Hezekiah and King Lemuel also occur. This is just one indication that, as in the east generally, this kind of teaching was thought beneficial in the education of princes and administrators. With the cultivation of writing and fine language it combined development of character and behaviour. Kings like Solomon would foster schools of wisdom, and indeed would wish themselves to be considered sages, able to compose words of guidance.

The connection with government does not mean that the teachings would be a kind of early Civil Service manual. The ancient point of view was that government in society depended on the divine order that animated all creation. What rulers were desired to learn, first and foremost, was the way of right and truth in harmony with this cosmic order – and this is the fundamental concern of Proverbs.

From the time of Solomon especially (c. 960 BC), this tradition of schooling will have been developed in Israel and so continued down the centuries. At the outset the sages or teachers were able to make use of far older traditions, especially from Egypt, adapting them as necessary to the religion and culture of Israel. The main adaptation was to make it clear that the cosmic order was the work of the one God, known in Israel as 'Yahweh' (commonly rendered as 'the Lord'). Beyond this, however, their teaching remained remarkably non-national. It is expressed as valid for any person or society.

The teaching was valuable beyond the immediate task of training rulers, and would be eagerly sought and cherished by all who longed for the good way: a hard way indeed, but in the end the path of light and life, the way to the well of life. They would here find themselves addressed and trained by the sage as individuals, as a father might speak to his son.

The collections of teaching in Proverbs no doubt represent a harvest of several centuries. We would expect development over the years, shifts of emphasis, further reflection on particular topics. But modern scholars have perhaps been too quick to assume lines of development in the essential character of the tradition. It was often supposed that the tradition changed from a secular to a religious outlook, from advice for self-advancement to a piety of fearing God, from a wisdom that is only human skill to a divine Wisdom that seeks and blesses us, or from brief detached proverbs to longer poetic discourses. But many of the supposedly later characteristics match features of teaching far earlier than Hebrew wisdom, especially in Egypt. It is better, then, to think of the tradition in Proverbs as the unfolding of a philosophy and world-view which did not change in essentials.

The first collection (chapters 1–9) is characterized by extended treatments of a theme. The poetic form, as generally in ancient Hebrew, weaves patterns of ideas, often with balancing lines ('parallelism'). We notice at once favourite words in this stream of teaching: 'wisdom', 'instruction', 'discipline', 'insight', 'counsel', 'right (order)', 'the simple', 'the fool', and so on. We can feel our way into the meaning of such terms as we gain familiarity with the material.

From chapter 10 onwards we have collections of short sayings, still in poetry. Each saying needs much pondering. No doubt the sage himself expected his disciple to consider a saying deeply, sometimes meditating on it for hours and finding in it promptings for many reflections. Certainly the sage saw no good in sayings used glibly, but not thought through:

> Limp hang the legs of the lame,
> and a proverb from the mouth of fools.
>
> 26.7

The words of the sages were said to be 'goads', stimulating to new levels of awareness (Ecclesiastes 12.11). But sharp indeed were they against those who used them without discretion:

> A brier comes into the clutch of a drunk,
> and a proverb into the mouth of fools.
>
> Prov. 26.9

Rounding off the short sayings is a concluding longer poem portraying a valiant wife; it is an acrostic, each line beginning with the next letter of the alphabet.

The book is thus not one to read long and swiftly. Used thoughtfully, it becomes a doorway into the world of eastern wisdom. Here are disciples who gladly take on a yoke of discipline to sit at the feet of a sage. And here are teachers who carry forward the insights of generations of sages, but who desire for each disciple personal awareness and judgment. We are welcome to pass through the doorway, sit with them, and grow in heart and understanding.

The Book of Job

This seems to be an early kind of drama.[3] It dates perhaps from between the seventh and fifth centuries BC, but draws upon much more ancient tradition of wisdom, story and song. The prologue and epilogue are prose narrative, and probably follow the lines of a traditional tale of a righteous sufferer. Within this framework flows a succession of poetic speeches by Job and his well-meaning but quite vexing consolers, and at last by God. In these speeches the dramatic action consists chiefly in the growth of Job's appeal to God and God's eventual appearance. The rising tension between Job and his vexatious counsellors makes an effective supporting action, exposing the perplexities of human life which baffle human understanding.

The design of the great author is best appreciated when account is taken of two main changes which his work seems to have suffered in its history of use. The first affects the third round of discussion, chapters 22–27. Here there has been some loss and dislocation of material. One friend's speech is cut short (25.6), another's (Zophar's) is missing (27.1), while some of their words may have found their way into Job's speeches (26.5–14; 27.7–23).

The second change, in all probability, was the insertion of an extra counsellor, Elihu, who delivers four speeches without interruption (32–37). It seems that, while the work was still used in dramatic recital or enactment, it was felt necessary to add this character to adjust the balance of the teaching. Elihu criticizes Job's stance in a rather harsh manner and develops the inappropriate idea that suffering contains a warning from God, giving a chance for repentance. Someone must have felt strongly that all this needed saying. Fortunately the great poet's ending remains, with God in the epilogue pronouncing Job in the right without qualification. If these changes in the author's work have obscured his design, making it somewhat ambiguous, they have hardly diminished the power of the drama to stimulate meditation.

Some scholars have taken the great poet to be a rebel against the traditional wisdom. On this view the sages are represented by the three counsellors, who speak impressively but are brought down with a crash at the end. The author then utters his rebellious thoughts through Job, who shows how injustice reigns everywhere.

But it is better to think of the author as expressing a facet of the tradition. The contradictions of life which concern him had long been considered in eastern philosophy. Treatments, sometimes in dialogue form, are known from the Euphrates valley, Egypt and India.[4] Questioning contributions could always be made within the tradition. There was room for lively debate.

Our author was in fact in line with the old teaching that wisdom was not to be applied in an unthinking manner, without genuine observation and discernment. He exposes Job's friends as guilty of this error, deficient in real concern for truth and so for God.

Through the character of Job he expresses a noble ideal. Here is someone who held to truth, trusting in an ultimate goodness, when everything conspired against him. Job could be satisfied with nothing less than God. He was then rewarded in a mysterious and surprising way by the disclosure of God to him in the very abyss of his suffering.

With its undogmatic form of story and drama, the work is in the true tradition of wisdom as 'goad' to further reflection. Here is no set of answers to life's problems. But the spectator is drawn into an experience which purifies and strengthens in the good way to God. And not least remarkable is the disclosure of God through contemplative wonder (38–41). Divine wisdom, beauty and love are revealed in contemplation of skies, seas, animals, and through it all God himself is known. Job sees God immediate – and would lose himself, sorrowful and yet at peace (42.5–6).[5]

As in the case of Proverbs, we are struck by the non-national character of the book. We hear of the one God, Creator and Ruler, though only in the prologue and epilogue is he normally, in Israelite fashion, called 'Yahweh'. Otherwise there is no reference to distinguishing features of Israelite religion, unless we count the abhorrence of worship of sun and moon (31.26–28). The characters belong to the people dwelling on the fringe of the Syro-Arabian desert, tribesmen of the 'Children of the East'. The issues are presented as universal.

Ecclesiastes

This remarkable work, one of the Old Testament's big

surprises, reminds us of those modern plays for one actor. The modern actor, perhaps seated simply on stage at a table, takes the part of a character with experiences to relate and relive, to ponder and evaluate. The audience are closely engaged, as in a deep conversation, and from the particular experiences told them are led to think again about the nature of life, with all its hopes and disappointments.

Ecclesiastes is quite like such a play. As its language indicates, it was composed about the third century BC. The author brings on to his imaginary stage the fabulous King Solomon from the tenth century BC. He has the king speak at length of his experiences of life and his search for its value. He speaks as the man who has had everything generally deemed desirable: wealth, wisdom, women, power, achievement. He can assess from first-hand knowledge the value and vanity of it all.

The author has given his character beautiful lines, passing almost imperceptibly between poetry and melodious prose. The thoughts have a personal air, often beginning 'I saw', 'I considered', or 'I said to myself'. But while they express the author's own observations, they are rooted in deep antiquity. Discussions of life's value that are sober to the point of pessimism are known from ancient Egypt and Mesopotamia.[6]

Although the author has effectively used the dramatic device of the character of King Solomon, he has lifted him from his immediate history to be a counsellor to all ages. He has the king make a few allusions to grand activities, wealth and pursuit of wisdom, but otherwise there is no use of the history of Solomon. Even his name is avoided. Instead the king calls himself 'Qohelet' (traditionally rendered 'the Preacher' and in the title, 'Ecclesiastes'). Perhaps the word denotes the office of a great 'assembler' – one who gathered and addressed the people, or one who gathered wise sayings.

A main theme is heard at the outset. It will recur often:

> Vanity of vanities, says Qohelet,
> vanity of vanities, all is vanity.

The word translated 'vanity' (*hebel*) suggests a puff of air, mere vapour. Sometimes our book uses it clearly to refer to the apparent absurdities of life: incongruous, senseless things.

The philosopher-king, who has enjoyed all the world has to offer, thus declares it all insubstantial, fleeting, unsatisfying, incongruous.

A play sounding only this theme from beginning to end would itself have rather a short run. But this work still weaves its spell after thousands of years. It is exactly an author of such clear-minded honesty, turned with open face to life's tragedy, who can move us when he finds value after all.

Inevitably, some scholars have attempted to separate the strands of 'disillusion' and 'faith' in the book, ascribing them to different writers. It is true that touches by an editor may reasonably be detected in a few places, such as the last six verses and the last sentence of 11.9. But the main bitter-sweet texture should be accepted, as indeed the unity of the author's experience. His joy in the light given in the midst of great darkness is as precious as Job's faith amidst bitter outrage. It is in such contexts that the ultimate discovery is made.

Ecclesiasticus

Jesus ben Sira lived around 200 BC. His Hebrew book of wisdom was translated into Greek in Egypt by his grandson in 132 BC, with the addition of an interesting preface about the task. This whole Greek work became part of the scriptures of the early church. Although many chapters of the Hebrew text have come to light from Cairo and sites by the Dead Sea, it did not attain a place in the Hebrew Bible, perhaps because of its known late origin. As a result, the Protestant churches reckon it among the Apocrypha. Its name Ecclesiasticus, 'the church (book)', is from the Latin Bible, suggesting its usefulness in the ancient church. It is indeed a lively, excellent work, gathering up much from the old wisdom, and also showing the confluence of that old stream with the piety of later Judaism.

Like Proverbs, it is poetry. Short sayings are grouped according to theme, and there are extended passages of teaching on particular subjects. There is an interesting range of topics, including relations between friends and in family life, worries with daughters, money matters, mourning customs, manners in society, dangers of the tongue, the uses of physicians, sketches of other employments. Often the sage's love of God finds expression in passages of praise and thanksgiving.

Ben Sira shares the view of the old wisdom that the teaching furthers the training of those who would administer and govern. From his school would come disciples able to serve among great men, appear before princes, undertake missions abroad, always testing the good and evil among people (39.4). Through respect for the sages and deep study of their sayings, one became fitted for office (8.8).

An important theme carried forward from Proverbs is the presentation of 'Wisdom' as a gracious divine being. She represents the breath or utterance of God at the beginning of creation, giving order and fruitfulness (24.3). But at this point the supra-national character of the old teaching recedes. This Wisdom, according to Ben Sira, was given a resting place in Jerusalem and ministered in the holy shrine (24.10–12). She is further explained as the law which Moses commanded, the book of the covenant of the most high God (24.23). The wise man is one who keeps these commandments. Great figures of Israelite history and the current high priest are praised (44–50).

At these points, then, we see an integration of wisdom and Jewish piety more obvious than anything in the books already discussed. Even so, much of the character of the old inheritance is still clear to see in Ben Sira's eloquent work.

The Sayings of the Fathers

The Jewish Mishna was completed about AD 200. An assemblage of sixty-three tractates, it recorded teachings and discussions that had been handed down orally, chiefly concerning the application of the Law of Moses. It was accepted as authoritative, being regarded as the product of an oral tradition of interpretation reaching back in an unbroken chain to the first teachers.

Among these tractates is one called Aboth, or Pirqe Aboth, commonly known as The Sayings of the Fathers.[7] It is the only one to be included in the Jewish prayer book, and is read in synagogue on a succession of sabbaths. It is remarkably different in character from the other tractates, being chiefly a collection of maxims relevant to moral and religious life in general.

The sayings are sometimes anonymous, but many are ascribed to named teachers stretching back several centuries before the compilation. They lead us above all into the circles of sages and disciples a little later than Ben Sira. The subject of study by now is definitely *tora*, the revelation to Moses and its flowing on through the dedicated work of teaching and study. But the Sayings are still helpful to our consideration of the old wisdom. The teachers are still called 'the wise', the sages, and the methods and attitudes in their circles still carry forward much from the ancient sages. The way to the divine order and to God appeared to the later sages as centred in the study of *tora*, but they are like the ancient teachers in their commitment to a way that brings them nearer to the One who gives all life.

The last chapter of the Sayings, chapter 6, was added several centuries after the others. It thus carries us still further down the tradition of Hebraic wisdom and closer to the flowering of Jewish mysticism in the Middle Ages.

In the works just surveyed we shall be able to enjoy the main part of the Old Testament wisdom tradition and make fruitful comparison with the world's contemplative writings. Subsequently we shall consider psalms affected by currents of wisdom. But now our introductory chapter must continue with a sketch of world writings that will feature in our comparisons.

Egypt

The ancient Egyptian wisdom writings are often similar to the Israelite and are in themselves very impressive. The favourite form is of advice given by a king or senior statesman to his son and successor. One of the earliest is presented as the guidance given by the vizier Ptah-hotep (about 2450 BC) to his son at the direction of the king. Now that the vizier is old, his son must be ready to succeed, duly prepared in the control of speech, in love of justice, in modesty, discretion, awareness of the divine order in life, and so forth. At the outset this early text reminds us of one of the latest in the Old Testament, Ecclesiastes 12. The vizier tells the king:

> O sovereign, my lord! Oldness has come; old age has descended. Feebleness has arrived; dotage is coming anew. The heart sleeps wearily every day. The eyes are weak, the ears are deaf, the strength is disappearing because of weariness of heart, and the mouth is silent and cannot speak. The heart is forgetful and cannot recall yesterday. The bone suffers old age. Good is become evil. All taste is gone . . . The nose is stopped up and cannot breathe. To stand up or to sit down is difficult.[8]

The instruction proper begins with a theme basic also in Israelite wisdom:

> Let not your heart be puffed up because of your knowledge,
> be not confident because you are a wise man.

> Good speech is more hidden than the emerald,
> but it may be found with maidservants at the grindstone.[9]

Another great text is the instruction given to King Merikare by his father (c. 2180 BC). There is a reckoning here with the brevity of earthly life, judgment and eternity. There must be respect for a life of attentiveness, 'open of face'. There must be reverence for the Creator who has given the breath of life in the nostrils and begotten men in his image.

Some compositions are especially concerned with the education of the scribe, comparing this high vocation favourably with other crafts and trades. It is a theme which Ben Sira was to take up in his own way nearly 2000 years later (Ecclus. 38–39). Still before the time of Solomon, the instruction of Ani to his son insists on quietness. The dwelling of God abominates clamour. The prayer hidden deep in the heart is acceptable. One must not ask rashly about the form of God. The young man should recognize his wife's efficiency. He should not demand, 'Where is such and such? Fetch it!' A little more silence and he would have seen that she had already put it in the best place.

It is notable that it is one of the latest texts (Onchsheshonqy, c. 400 BC) that has the earthiest tone and least refined form. It includes reflection on the order of nature and touchingly prays, 'O may life always succeed death'.

Of particular significance for our study is the Egyptian concept of Maat, 'order', 'truth', 'justice', personified as a female divinity.[10] She is the thought of the Creator's heart and the utterance of his mouth. She is his companion, his daughter, and she is represented in the form of a girl bearing a feather on her head as a symbol of holiness. She is the very life and food of gods and men, and the king is represented as offering a little image of her on the palm of his hand stretched out to the Creator. The association of the Creator and Maat has its counterpart in the king and his sister-bride. On earth the king alone directly knows Maat and her requirements. He is pledged to love her and abhor her opposite: chaos and falsehood. From his knowledge of Maat he issues laws which uphold order in the world and society. Maat's laws are never fully and finally revealed. She herself is unchanged since the beginning of things, but each king interprets her requirements as befits his time. His rules and teachings, as also the ancient teachings of the wise, thus serve the cause of Maat, are an offering up of Maat and sustain the world.

The administrators, trained in wisdom, are especially charged to be her devotees. Their head, the Vizier, is titled 'Prophet of Maat' and wears her image under the garment round his neck. Those who love Maat will find that she does not leave them at death. She takes part in the trial of the dead and vindicates those whose hearts have been true and, being weighed against her feather, are not heavy with misdeeds.

Maat is said to have come out from heaven in the beginning and become companion to those who dwell on earth. Through her the first society was healthy and joyful. Nature gave in plenty, walls did not collapse nor thorns prick. Altogether, Maat is the principal divine power, the order and goodness which is the essence of the divine creation, the foundation and former of cosmic and social life. And from her and for her is all the flow of ancient Egyptian wisdom.

China

As we approach the contemplative themes of Israelite wisdom, we shall often find it fruitful to refer to the sages of ancient China. The most famous of all, Confucius (c. 551–479

BC), is sometimes regarded as an agnostic or a humanist, but his ethical teaching can be shown to rest upon awareness of a universal, divine order.[11] He is said to have remarked that only Heaven truly knew him; Heaven had a purpose in him which no oppressor could frustrate. The best source for his teaching, as it passed into the first circles of his disciples, is a collection of brief dialogues and proverbial sayings. His ideal society was a hierarchy embracing heaven and earth in a family spirit. The prescriptions for good behaviour (*li*) sustained proper roles and relationships within this great family, and so drew society into harmony with the *tao*, the 'way', the universal order. Believing that ideal order had prevailed in society under the early kings, he invested his scholarly study of the past with profound reverence.

A reaction to later Confucian tradition came with the remarkable Mo-tzu (c. 480–390 BC). By now, it seemed to him, the Confucians had become lethargic and greedy. He taught a love which went out in remedial action. This was the way to work with Heaven and establish the good order.

This programme of purposive action seems to have generated deeper reflection on the divine order which human effort fails to storm. Whether or not there was a historical Lao-tzu – a hermit known to Confucius, or a sage of the following century – the little work that goes under this name offers in paradoxical style some of the world's greatest sayings in the contemplative spirit. True, some interpreters see it only as prudential counsel, moral rather than mystical, commending meekness as the most practical path to survival.[12] But thirty of the eighty-one sections are reasonably taken by others to treat the mystery underlying experience, and the whole teaching fits with a contemplative awareness, a vision of all-pervading reality.[13]

Here the order or 'way' (*tao*) in society and nature that can be readily discerned is made possible by an infinitely more mysterious Tao, the ultimate reality beyond naming or description. The path of *wu-wei*, 'non-action', is the avoidance of aggressive, self-sufficient action; it is the way of sensitivity to the great Tao, an alignment with the true order, what the Old Testament might call 'waiting upon the Lord'. It is not considered a counsel for retiring from the concerns of the world. On the contrary it is presented as the only effective way of government. Only sage-kings who have fully entered into this way can save their people from the ills of corrupt civilization.[14]

Greek wisdom

The great Plato (428–348 BC) was also desirous of contemplative rulers. In his analysis of the human condition, the soul had to find again what it once knew. It had to come home to the eternal, divine order from which it had grown distant. By contemplation (*theoria*) of the eternally true, beautiful and good, it could be joined again to them.[15] Plato's teaching was to flow on through several great successors to become a rich heritage of the Christian church.

An important link between Plato and the church was Philo of Alexandria (c. 20 BC – after AD 41).[16] This Jewish scholar expounded the scriptures (Genesis to Deuteronomy) in the context of Greek philosophy. He stresses that God in himself is unknowable, but mediates knowledge of himself through his outgoing work of rule and blessing. To such revelation of God we respond with contemplation, the unsleeping eye of the mind, sustained by constant yearning for wisdom and a discipline of purity.

A fresh exposition and organization of Plato's teaching was given by Plotinus (AD 204–270) with great influence on Christian thought. From the Absolute, the One, all emanates and is intended to return. The way of return is a movement of desire, developed and expressed in contemplation. All things strive for contemplation and vision, each attaining in its own way and degree. The ascent to the One is not a climbing upward and outward, but an entering more deeply within oneself.[17]

Meanwhile Christian writers were carrying forward their rich biblical inheritance in the world of teaching stemming from Greek philosophy. For Irenaeus (Bishop of Lyons from AD 170) perfect life is to see God, who has become visible in Christ. The path of discipleship leads gradually from feeble and indirect vision to the life of eternity and full seeing.[18]

Platonic influence is marked in the great biblical commentator Origen (AD 185–254). He shares the notion of the return to God by and for contemplation, but relates it to the soul's union with Christ the Word. For him the Old Testament books attributed to Solomon corresponded to stages on the way to full contemplation. Proverbs was a guide to right and disciplined living. Ecclesiastes gave insight into the vanity of earthly ambitions and desires and showed where good was to be found. The Song of Songs expressed the dialogue of love between the soul and the divine Word: communion with God, perfect contemplation. [19]

The Desert Fathers

Practical consequences of the desire for contemplation in the early church are evidenced in the withdrawal of some to the deserts west of the Nile delta. While our sources do not spring direct from these hermits and disciples, they still give insight into the ways of these pioneers, who greatly influenced subsequent Christian monastic movements. In the *Sayings of the Desert Fathers* we have especially the situation of disciples visiting masters for words of guidance, on which they would then meditate in solitude. [20] The counsel was above all an encouragement in the way of humility and the fear of God. The most rigorous way of life was still to be subject to the rule of love. Work was valued; the 'life of labour' and the 'life of the heart' must be joined in fruitful relationship. [21]

Denys

During a controversy in the sixth century AD some writings were brought forward which, though certainly not from the New Testament Dionysius/Denys (Acts 17.34) as claimed, proved very influential in later centuries. The author may have been a fifth-century Syrian and is still most conveniently referred to as Denys. His spiritual path is a three-fold process of purification, illumination, and perfection or union. The second stage here involves contemplation of the world in God and of God's manifestation of himself in creation. The third stage is a progress into darkness through negation: a withdrawal from the lesser, fragmentary world of the senses, a

knowing of God through unknowing, a loving union.[22]
Among the many influenced by Denys were some of the
English mystics of the fourteenth century, especially the
unknown author of *The Cloud of Unknowing* and Walter Hilton
(died 1396). In that remarkable century came also Mother
Julian of Norwich, who so movingly expressed her discovery
of the love of God.

Spanish contemplatives

The writings of St Teresa of Avila and St John of the Cross have
a special authority in the study of contemplation. These brave
Carmelites of sixteenth-century Spain showed in their lives as
well as in their writings a rare devotion to their Lord. Teresa's
writings overflow with the fullness of her personal experience
of God. John's experience is integrated with his high poetic
gifts and a well-trained theological mind. For comparison with
our Hebrew books it is especially significant that both saints
had a fundamental grasp of the unity of the human person,
body and soul being wholly interdependent.[23] Prayer, according to Teresa, was not a matter of thinking a great deal, but of
loving a great deal. On the path of contemplation, she taught,
the prerequisites were love for one another, detachment from
desire of created things, and humility. Especially in the
imagery of night and darkness, John expressed the need of a
detachment from all that is not God, if union with God is to be
known. When desiring to possess nothing, one comes in him
to possess all.[24]

The Sufis of Islam

In the territories conquered by Islam, from the Mediterranean
to India, contemplative traditions lived on. Within Islam itself
the life of sprirtual discipline on the path to direct experience
of God soon began to flower, especially from the tenth to the
twelfth centuries. Those dedicated to this ideal were recognizable from their simple garments of wool (*suf*) and so became
known as Sufis. In view of the origin of Islam in the revelations
experienced by the prophet Muhammad, it was not difficult to
claim that the roots of the movement were in the Quran.

Tension arose between the established authorities of the faith and some Sufis, as when Hallaj was executed on a charge of blasphemy in AD 922. But when the militant community began to lose confidence, there was a great turning to Sufis who could be recognized as personally close to God. The twelfth century saw a great proliferation of groups attached to some acknowledged sage of the spiritual life.[25]

Jewish mystics

We have already noted that the Jewish Sayings of the Fathers reflects a contemplative wisdom centred on meditative study of *tora*. For some thousand years following, a Jewish mystical tradition centred on Ezekiel's vision of the divine chariot, the Merkaba (Ezekiel 1), but always the engagement with *tora* continued. By concentration and the 'directing' of the heart (the practice of *kawwana*), obedience to the laws was made into a continual recollection of God, an abiding with him. As the mystic 'tradition' (*qabbala*) developed in Spain and Provence in the twelfth and thirteenth centuries, not only the *tora* was seen as the cosmic plan; the human being also, as in the image of God, is intimately related to the universe in which God has revealed himself. Thus the sages cultivated a strong sense of the interactive unity of creation and of the significance of every deed.[26] This piety was well represented from the sixteenth century among the masters dwelling in Saphed, Galilee.

Constant 'cleaving' or 'adhering' to God (*debequt*) was a central concern of the Hasidic movement (*hasid* = *'faithful'*) initiated in Eastern Europe by Israel Baal Shem Tob (1698–1760). This popular piety, still flourishing today, looks for guidance to sages called 'the righteous' (*saddiq*), and from such inspiring figures have grown various forms of devotion.

India

The relevance of India to our undertaking is already apparent when we read this characterization of Indian wisdom by R. L. Slater:

For the Hindu, the way of salvation is the way of knowledge, but what is sought is not knowledge *about* reality, but
knowledge *of* reality; a knowledge which is awareness; a
knowledge by acquaintance. Hence an emphasis on intuition and the fact that Hindu sages are significantly described as those who *see* the truth.[27]

For our present purpose it must suffice briefly to situate some
sources that will later call for mention.

In the foremost division of Hindu scriptures (the *śruti*, 'That
which has been heard') are the four collections of mystical
'knowledge', the Vedas, consisting of poetic hymns, blessings
and other chants. Dating from perhaps 1500–1000 BC, they
were passed down orally for centuries and so guarded from
unauthorized persons. The Vedas begot other works of
commentary and discourse, first the Brahmanas and then the
Upanishads. Of these last there are more than 250, of which
about fifteen have special importance and antiquity (from
c. 700 BC). 'Upanishad' means 'sitting down close' and reflects
the situation of master and disciple; the material is a sample of
what was passed down and guarded in various ashrams or
monasteries. Some is prose and some poetry; the names of the
teachers are sometimes preserved.[28]

In the secondary grouping of Hindu scriptures (the *smríti*,
'That which is remembered') comes the famous 'Song of the
Lord', the Bhagavad Gita, perhaps from the fourth century
BC. This poetic Upanishad is incorporated into the vast epic
poem of the Mahabharata, said to be the longest poem in the
world, the story of a war. The Gita has the form of a
conversation between the god Krishna and the warrior
Arjuna, and the war they refer to becomes symbolic of the
path to enlightenment. A special importance of the Gita is that
it brings together the adoration of God as a personal being and
the experience of the divine as the all-pervading Absolute.[29]

Gautama, the Buddha ('enlightened one'), lived and taught
in northern India about the sixth century BC. Having renoun-
ced his princely position, he became a wandering ascetic,
seeking higher truth. The traditional asceticism, bordering on
starvation, proved fruitless, but finding his own way of
contemplation, he at last experienced enlightenment. His first

sermon presents his insights as the 'four noble truths': recognition of sorrow everywhere, its cause as craving or covetousness, its cure as release from craving, and the eightfold path to release. The eightfold way consists in 1. 'right understanding' – insight into the nature, cause and cure of life's sorrow, 2. 'right thought' – orientation to good values, 3. 'right speech' – truthful, sparing, beneficent, 4. 'right action' – no killing, stealing, sexual abuse, 5. 'right livelihood' – wholesome trade or profession, 6. 'right effort' – genuine endeavour and perseverance, 7. 'right attentiveness' – control of the mind towards the good end, 8. 'right meditation' – the advanced stage of recollectedness, finding peace and illumination on the threshold of Nirvana (the ultimate peace when the flames of craving are overcome).[30]

This was the essence of his 'Middle Way' between the extremes of sensuality and mortification, a way that balanced discipline with a sane engagement with common life. Gautama felt moved to share his enlightenment widely and founded a monastic order to spread the teaching. He founded an order for women also, and accepted laypeople as disciples.

The Indian poet Kabir (born c. AD 1455) has been claimed by both Hindus and Muslims, but declared himself neither. He sang scathingly about the pretensions of religious pundits and ritualists. He was said to have been a Hindu, found and brought up by a Muslim weaver (and so of the lowest caste), to have sat at the feet of a Hindu sage, to have been imprisoned, thrice in danger of execution, exiled, and yet to have lived to a very great age. His songs were compact poetry, often just a couplet, and were transmitted by minstrels. His favourite theme is the love of God, the One who is everywhere, and deep within, the being of our being, the soul of our soul, beyond – and oh, so near. He is realistic about sorrow, the crushing between grindstones which none escape; realistic too about death. But he finds supreme joy in loving union with the Beloved within.[31]

Near and in our own time

Evelyn Underhill (1875–1941) introduced many English readers to the great writers of the Christian contemplative tradition in her major work *Mysticism* (1911, 1940) and other more popular writings. In early life she had little connection with the church. Visits to Italy aroused her: 'a discovery of art, history and religion all in one'.[32] Though attracted to Rome, it was to the Church of England that she returned positively in 1919. From the Catholic tradition she still derived much through taking Baron von Hügel as her spiritual guide. In her last years she contributed much to the growing fellowship of Anglicans and Orthodox. Writing with great clarity and reasonableness, she had a rare gift for perceiving and drawing together the essential threads of mystical experience. T. S. Eliot said she was inspired by a consciousness of the grievous need of the contemplative element in the modern world.[33]

But how can the ancient ways of wisdom and discipline be trodden with integrity in our time? One who lived out the quest in his own life and who wrote of it with grace was Thomas Merton (1915–1968). At the age of twenty-six he entered the silent Trappist order in America. His death by an accident on his first visit to the East came when he had already drunk deep of eastern wisdom. His various writings reflect successive stages of his journey along the contemplative path. All in all they draw together for us the wisdom of centuries of spiritual experience as tested and reshaped in his own agony and joy.[34]

Another light of wisdom in our day is Bede Griffiths (born 1906).[35] Formerly a monk of Prinknash Abbey and prior of Farnborough Abbey, he went to India in 1955 and helped in the foundation of an ashram-monastery in Kerala. Later he joined the Christian community living in the manner of a Hindu ashram by the sacred river Cavery. It is an open, hospitable prayer-centre where the wisdom traditions of East and West can give and receive in humility, love and prayer. Here again is a writer well rooted in his own tradition, but with the heart to recognize and rejoice in the same light burning in other lamps.

Such, then, in outline, are the main sources that will be at hand to compare with the wisdom of the Old Testament. They are but a sample of the world's wisdom treasures, but should be sufficient to illumine our appreciation of the old Hebrew sages.

2

THEMES OF WISDOM AND CONTEMPLATION

We shall now consider themes of contemplation one by one. On each theme we shall listen first to some of the world's contemplatives, and so be ready to hear more keenly what the Hebrew wisdom books have to say. Our first theme suggests the beginning of the disciple's way, and our last theme the end; but in practice all the themes intertwine with no beginning and no end.

The spiritual director

Everywhere there is insistence on the need for a spiritual director, master, 'father' or 'mother'. A striking example is offered by the Sufis of Islam. Seekers of wisdom would attach themselves to a guide, a master who commanded their obedience. They would sit with him and travel with him. As the movement grew, the disciples were organized in communities. Benefactors would endow dwelling-houses attached to a mosque. The premises would include a central kitchen, a school, a place for guests, and sometimes the tomb of the first master. While some of the seekers lived there, wholly dedicated to study and meditation under the close daily supervision of the master, others came in for the times of devotion and then returned to their outside occupations.

The Sufi director guided his pupils on a 'way' (*tariqa*) of training and devotion, and each school or order (also *tariqa*) was known by the way it followed. It was said, 'Whoever travels without a guide needs two hundred years for a two days' journey.' The accounts present the typical master as 'a robust and vigorous man, full of life, paradox and humour'. The would-be disciple might find himself rebuffed and tested by years of waiting to be accepted.[1]

In ancient India some of the sages went teaching from village to village, but others established schools, sitting with their pupils in regular dialogue. The rough but caring work of the director or guru is caught by Kabir thus:

> The guru
> Is a potter
> And the pupil
> A pot.
> How it hurts
> When he thumps
> From the outside,
> But see
> How delicately
> He supports
> From the inside,
> So a beautiful pot
> May be created.[2]

Among the sayings ascribed to the Chinese sage Lao-tzu is one which reflects the respect given to the guide, and not only by beginners:

> He who neither values his teacher
> nor loves the lesson
> is one gone far astray,
> however learned he may be.[3]

The 'way' in China (the 'Tao') had still deeper meanings: the very goal of the contemplative path, the fundamental reality of the universe. A case is recounted where a sage taught a disciple 'how to get Tao'. Patiently he waited and watched with him, guiding him through progressive stages, each taking a number of days, until at last he attained security amidst the world's confusion.[4]

Confucius considered himself to be not a sage but 'one in love with ancient studies'. He never turned away anyone who came earnestly to learn. But he expected response and initiative:

> I will not explain to one who is not trying to make things clear to himself. And if I explain a quarter and the man does not go back and reflect and think over the implications in the remaining three quarters for himself, I will not bother to teach him again.[5]

Confucius was fortunate in one of his disciples, who was said by fellow-students to need 'but to understand one part in order to understand all ten parts'.[6] Mo-tzu trained his novices by having them dress simply like labourers and eat only a daily meal of vegetable soup. When they had completed his course and taken up their work in the world as officials, he still regarded them as owing him obedience.[7]

The early Christian solitaries in the Egyptian desert recognized the importance of a master. They would group themselves round an 'abba', according him the obedience of sons. It was said, 'If you see a young man climbing up to heaven by his own will, seize him by the foot and pull him down, for this will be to his profit.'[8]

There are interesting recollections of how these revered Desert Fathers dispensed their counsel. The gist of many questions put to them was 'What shall I do to be saved?' To one such enquirer Abba Euprepius replied, rather pointedly we may think, 'If you wish to be saved, when you go to see someone, do not speak until you are spoken to.'[9] A glimpse of a study group comes in another story, where the students, including Abba Joseph, sat at the feet of Abba Anthony. The master put before them some scripture and asked each in turn for its meaning, beginning with the youngest. As each gave the best answer he could, the old man said, 'You have not understood it'. Last he came to Abba Joseph, whose answer was, 'I do not know'. The master declared, 'Truly Abba Joseph has found the way, for he has said, I do not know'.[10]

Situations of spiritual guidance and teaching are often apparent in Old Testament wisdom. There is an interesting example in Isaiah 40.13–14. In affirming that the Creator needed no teacher, the prophet uses some interesting language of education. His phrases presuppose the sage who would 'regulate the spirit' of the pupil; he would be his 'counsellor' and 'cause him to know'; he would 'counsel' his pupil to 'impart discernment' and 'teach him in the path of order (or justice)'; he would 'teach him knowledge' and 'cause him to know the way of understanding'. It was obviously not just a course in factual learning!

In Proverbs the sage often addresses an individual disciple, 'my son' (1.8, 10; 2.1, etc.), and occasionally a group, 'sons' (4.1). The subject of instruction sometimes implies that the disciples are grown men, even fathers (23.13, 22). He recommends them to consort with the wise and become wise (13.20). They should set their heart on the knowledge he imparts and keep his sayings, deeply meditated, in their belly, ready for use on their lips (22.17f).

Like a true father, the sage in Proverbs delights in the progress of a good novice:

> My son, if your heart becomes wise,
> my heart too will rejoice,
> and my inward being will exult
> when your lips speak right.
>
> 23.15f.

Like a father also he felt he could appeal for personal trust and sincere respect:

> My son, give your heart to me
> and let your eyes approve my ways.
>
> 23.26

So the disciple would learn the 'way' of wisdom, avoiding many traps and temptations (23.19). The fatherly sage knows that what he offers is supremely good and so, in the end, delightful:

> Eat, my son, honey, for it is good,
> the honeycomb is sweet in your mouth.
> Know that thus is wisdom to your soul.
> If you find her, you can expect good,
> and your hope will not be dashed.
>
> 24.13f.

Perhaps from the benefit of tutorial debate and mutual care arose these insights:

> Iron is sharpened on iron,
> and each man sharpens the face of his fellow.
> Whoever guards well a fig-tree will eat its fruit,
> and whoever watches his master will get
>   honour.
>
> 27.17f.

These were circles where the wise listened carefully, testing words as the palate tests food, discerning right for themselves, judging what was good within their own debate (Job 34.2f.).

The Hebrew tradition of the fatherly sage and spiritual director lives on in Jesus ben Sira, though he feels he comes late in a long line, with little new to offer:

> I was the last on watch,
> a gleaner following the grape-gatherers.
>
> Ecclus. 33.16

He would tend his disciples as a gardener a rose, looking for a beautiful flower giving off wisdom's fragrance:

> Listen to me, devout sons,
> and bud like a rose growing by a channel of water.
> Give fragrance like frankincense
> and blossom like a lily.
>
> 39.13f.

Ben Sira is the master of a 'house of research' (*bet midrashi*), and it is always open to the untaught to enter and lodge and receive the discipline of learning, the yoke of training, discovering the life of dedicated work, mercy and the praise of God (51.23–30). The master's example is the incentive:

> See with your own eyes how little was my toil
> compared with the great peace I have found.
>
> 51.27

In later Judaism the master's role remained greatly valued on the pilgrimage of truth. 'Get yourself a master': so you must begin, according to the Sayings of the Fathers (1.6). And when mature, your duty is plain: 'Raise up many disciples'

(1.1). What an honour if your house shelters a study-circle, what a privilege if you might sit with them!

> Let your house be a meeting-place for the wise,
> and get yourself all dusty with the dust of their feet,
> and thirstily drink up their words.
>
> 1.4

Like any good tutor, the sage well knew the qualities of each of his disciples. He came to recognize the various types: those who mopped up all they heard, those who received it by one ear and lost it by the other, and those who, in varying degrees, heard and retained with discrimination:

> Four characters of those who sit at the feet of the wise –
> the sponge, the funnel, the cullender, and the sieve.
>
> 5.18

The opinions of Johanan ben Zakkai on five of his disciples show affection and discernment of character. Of one he said, 'A plastered cistern, not losing a drop'; of another, 'Happy she who gave him birth'; of another, 'Faithful'; of another, 'Afraid to make a mistake'; and most admiringly of the last, 'A spring in full spate' (2.11). Evidently this sage, like Confucius, appreciated the student who had something to contribute.

Discipline and austerity

One of the functions of a spiritual director is to guide the novice into patterns of discipline and simplicity of life. Left to themselves, beginners flounder from one extreme to the other. The experienced sage can establish lines by which the disciple can develop the self-control necessary for the good ends in view. His judgment, too, can assess the degree of austerity needed to gain freedom of the spirit.

While the emphasis has varied, we may say that generally throughout the history of contemplation discipline and austerity have a valued place. Here are contemplatives settled beside a lake in first-century Egypt, described by Philo: 'They lay down self-control as a kind of foundation of the soul, and on this build the other virtues.'[11] And he goes on to tell of their simple attire and shelter. A classical Hindu pattern of life embraced both ascetic and worldly phases. The devotee might thus begin as a student of sacred knowledge, subsequently become a married householder until the birth of his grandchildren, and then retire to a life of solitude and meditation.[12] Kabir noted that professional ascetics were sometimes greedy, while householders could be 'free of all things'. He prayed:

> Grant me
> Just enough,
> O my Lord,
> So that all my family
> Is well served
> And none
> Who comes to my door
> For alms
> Is rebuffed![13]

Another great Indian tradition, Jainism, also embraced the life of both monks and laity with a discipline conducive to contemplation. The regime included vegetarianism, fasting, limitation to a fixed place, hospitality, and compassion for all living beings.[14]

The Chinese Taoists recognized a role for austerity in their quest for an ideal simplicity. The people's great enemy was assertive, feverishly active greed. Rather:

> Give them simplicity to look at,
> the uncarved block to hold,
> give them selflessness and fewness of desires.[15]

> To be hollow is to be filled,
> to be tattered is to be renewed,
> to have little is to possess,
> to have plenty is to be confused.[16]

The greatest folly was the lust for possessions:

> He who is contented with contentment
> will always be content.[17]

We meet here the same recommendation to forego travel and rushing hither and thither:

> Without stepping outside one's doors
> one can know everything under heaven,
> without looking out of one's windows
> one can see the Tao of heaven.
> The farther one travels,
> the less one knows.
> Therefore the sage knows without running about,
> understands without seeing,
> accomplishes without doing.[18]

The way to true being was the art of making the roots strike deep by fencing the trunk.[19] Such simplicity of life is valued also by Confucius:

> There is pleasure in lying against a bent arm after a meal of simple vegetables with a drink of water. But to enjoy wealth and power not gained through righteousness is to me like so many floating clouds.[20]

Old Testament wisdom laid a great stress on discipline. In Proverbs there is frequent praise of 'discipline' (*musar*) and 'reproof' (*tokaḥat*). Beyond insistence on the need for them in the upbringing of children, they are presented as essential to the whole life of wisdom. The very purpose of the book is to impart knowledge of 'wisdom and discipline' (1.2). Further:

> He who loves discipline loves knowledge.
>
> 12.1
>
> Hear counsel, receive discipline,
> that at last you become wise.
>
> 19.20
>
> Cease, my son, to hear discipline,
> only to stray from words of knowledge.
>
> 19.27
>
> He who observes discipline
> is on the path of life.
>
> 10.17

The theme is maintained strongly by Ben Sira. He tells how Wisdom first afflicts with her discipline (Ecclus. 4.17). The student must put his feet in her fetters and his neck in her collar (51.26). Even the sage still strives for the control that discipline gives:

> O that whips were set over my thoughts
> and Wisdom's discipline over my mind!
>
> 23.2

An aspect of discipline is the restraint of appetites. Often in Proverbs there is praise of a 'little' rather than abundance of goods. In such a life of 'little' the sage knows what it is to find space for the true values of life – quietness, love, fellowship, and knowledge of God's nearness:

> Better is a little with fear of the Lord
> than great store and all the trouble with it.
>
> Better a meal of vegetables and love with it
> than a fatted ox and strife with it.
>
> 15.16f.
>
> Better is a little with right
> than great income without justice.
>
> 16.8

For wisdom one should crave, not for gold and silver (16.16). One who staggers in the way of revelry and drunkenness cannot tread surely on the path of wisdom (20.1). Not that one should be abstemious to the point of self-destruction. As the Desert Fathers would later be careful to provide for their basic needs by making baskets for the market, so the wise man in Proverbs does not court total poverty. He prays to avoid penury and its temptations to steal, and likewise to avoid wealth and its temptations to godlessness:

> Two things I ask of you (Lord),
> do not deny me them before I die:
> Put far from me falsehood and lies,
> and give me neither poverty nor riches.
> Feed me just with the food necessary for me,
> lest I be well filled and deny you,
> saying, Who is the Lord?
> Or lest I be poor and steal,
> profaning the name of my God.
>
> 30.7f.

Instead of the roaming eye and the rushing hither and thither of the greedy, it is only necessary to be still and be satisfied with wisdom (17.24; 21.5).

In the same spirit Ben Sira contrasts a life of bare essentials and integrity with sumptuous banqueting at the cost of self-respect:

> The necessities of life are water and bread,
> and clothing and a house to cover one's nakedness.
>
> Ecclus. 29.21

> How ample is a little for a disciplined man!
> He goes to bed breathing easily.
>
> 31.19

A deeper note of austerity sounds from Qohelet, notwithstanding his counsel to rejoice. He values the experiences of darkness and sorrow:

> Better a day of death
> than a day of birth.
> Better to go to a house of mourning
> than a house of feasting.
> Better sorrow than laughter,
> for by sadness of countenance
> the heart is made glad.
> The heart of the wise is in the house of mourning,
> but the heart of fools is in the house of mirth.
> Better to hear the rebukes of the sage
> than be one who listens to the song of fools.
>
> Eccles. 7.1–5

All this is to value the quiet valley of humiliation, where one can meditate on long perspectives, the ends of things, and the virtues of patience and humility (7.8). Here one can contemplate the work of God in its dimensions of agony:

> Contemplate the work of God,
> for who is able to make straight
> what he has made crooked?
>
> 7.13

Usually addressing the male disciple, the Israelite sage did not include celibacy in his programme of austerity. Against the dangers of the 'strange' woman, the seductress, he warns strongly. She flatters her gullible prey, but her house slopes down to the land of death (Prov. 2.16f). Rather embrace Wisdom, worthy indeed of love, and she will protect you; say

to her, 'You are my sister' (7.4). The married sage, seeking
quietness for contemplation, might dread an incessantly
strident wife:

> Persistent splashing on a day of downpour
> and a quarrelsome wife are much the same.
>
> 27.15

> Better to live on the corner of the roof
> than to share the whole house with a quarrelsome wife.
>
> 21.9, 19; 25.24

How happy if the pair can share the spirit of contemplation:

> A silent wife is the gift of the Lord.
> Her disciplined soul is precious beyond all telling.
>
> Ecclus. 26.14

The general view of marriage is markedly positive. To find a
wife is to obtain grace from God (Prov. 18.22). The wise wife is
the best of all gifts – God's gift (19.14). She is a tower of
strength (*ḥayil*, 31.10, 17) and speaks wisdom and true love
(31.26). Qohelet's recommendations for holding fast to joy
and contentment amidst life's perplexities include his advice:

> Look upon life with the woman you love.
>
> Eccles. 9.9

Ben Sira, in spite of occasional anti-female sayings (Ecclus.
42.12–14), can be especially warm:

> Do not deny yourself a wise and good wife.
>
> 7.19

> A good wife is a great blessing,
> granted with the blessings for one who fears the Lord.
> Rich or poor, his heart is glad
> and in all circumstances his face is cheerful.
>
> 26.3–4

> Without a fence the property is plundered,
> without a wife a man wanders about and sighs.
>
> 36.25

For order in the home, and so a disciplined life, the sage's
heart warms with gratitude:

Like the sun rising in the heights of the Lord
is the beauty of a good wife in her well-ordered home.

26.16

The austerity which makes space for the cultivation of
wisdom is still advocated in the Sayings of the Fathers:

More flesh, more worms;
more wealth, more cares . . .
more *tora*, more life;
more wisdom, more counsel . . .

2.8

In the latest part of the work, the counsel is put starkly. A list
of virtues needed for gain in *tora*-study includes humility,
trust in the wise, acceptance of corrections (*yissorin*), recognizing one's place, love of reproofs (*tokaḥot*), bearing of the yoke
with companions. The disciple is to have little business, little
intercourse with the world, little indulgence (*ta'anug*), little
sleep:

A morsel with salt you shall eat,
and water by measure you shall drink,
and you shall lie upon the earth,
and you shall live a life of rigour (*ṣa'ar*)
labouring in *tora*.

6.4

Poetry

The artist is among the contemplatives. He or she knows the
way of dedication and the search for immediacy with truth.
Evelyn Underhill wrote in 1914:

The poet must take that living stuff direct from the field and
river . . . with an awe that admits not of analysis . . . (it is)
because his attitude to the universe is governed by the
supreme artistic virtues of humility and love, that poetry is
what it is . . . and I include in the sweep of the poetic art the
coloured poetry of the painter, and the wordless poetry of
the musician and dancer too.[21]

The emphasis, she says, of both mystic and artist, is directly on what is received, rather than on their own reaction to it and rearrangement of it.[22]

When the deep affinity of artist and mystic is recognized, it comes as no surprise that poetry, or prose verging on poetry, is the characteristic medium of expression for the contemplatives. Whether they give us pure poetry, like that of St John of the Cross, or poetic prose, like that of Lady Julian of Norwich, there is a quality of direct, simple experience, of love and awe and truth in the words, which is the very soul of poetry and art.

Most of the Indian spiritual classics are poetry. The Sufis of Islam included great poets. The Taoists were essentially poets in approach and expression. Plato ascribed decisive importance to poetry and music in the formation of character and health, bringing the rhythm and harmony of the divine order deep into the soul.[23] He would have understood Confucius, who was so struck with some beautiful music that for three months he forgot the taste of meat.[24] Confucius advised:

> Wake yourself up with poetry,
> strengthen yourself with right conduct,
> complete your training with music.[25]

Much of Kabir's legacy is in the form of small sung poems, couplets called sakhis, 'witnesses'. Full of suggestive allusion and concentrated word-play, they awaken the spiritual seeker 'like a call of a morning bird announcing dawn'.[26]

The poetic quality of Old Testament wisdom, even in translation, is a great delight. In Proverbs one is often struck by the concentrated quality, inviting meditation. This is readily apparent in the humorous characterizations of behaviour – the idler a-bed, the bargain-hunter in the market, the drunk:

> The idler says, A lion's in the street!
> A fierce lion in the alley!
>
> 26.13

> Bad, bad, says the buyer,
> and then goes off and boasts.
>
> 20.14

> Whose is the 'Oh', whose the 'Ugh',
> whose are the quarrels, whose the groaning?
> Who have wounds for nothing and bleary eyes?
> Those who linger over wine,
> those who draw deep from mixed liquor.
>
> 23.29f.

How concise the fundamental teaching!

> Buy truth and never sell –
> wisdom, discipline and insight.
>
> 23.23

The poet-sage is ready to warm to a theme and expand in glowing images:

> Love and truth – never let them go!
> Bind them on your throat,
> write them on the tablet of your heart . . .
>
> Do not become wise in your own eyes!
> Fear the Lord and avoid wrong-doing –
> it will be a cure to your navel
> and medicine for your bones.
>
> 3.5–8

Such a theme for poetic enthusiasm is the praise of Wisdom, and not least in the later books. Thus Ben Sira has Wisdom describe herself:

> I grew as a cedar of Lebanon,
> like a cypress on the slopes of Hermon,
> like a palm-tree in Engedi,
> like roses in Jericho,
> like a lovely olive in the field,
> like a plane-tree set by water.
> Like cassia and camel's thorn I shed scent of spices,
> like fine myrrh I was fragrant,
> like galbanum, onycha and stacte
> and like the odour of frankincense in the holy shrine . . .
>
> Ecclus. 24.13f.

Ben Sira is eloquent, too, at the sense of creativity, with the author's joy of finding the little he has to offer being multiplied in the giving:

I was like a channel led from a river,
a water-way into a garden.
I said, I will water my orchard
and soak my garden beds,
and see, my channel became a river,
and the river a sea!
I will make discipline bright like the dawn
and make it shine far and wide.
I will again pour out teaching like prophecy
and bequeath it to the generations to come.
See, I have laboured not only for myself,
but for all who seek Wisdom!

24.30f.

It is in poetry that the sages expressed their deepest experience of divine meaning in the world, personified as the
female Wisdom (Proverbs 8). Poetry alone could convey this
awesome and delightful truth. She calls to the busy throngs
in the concourse, commending wiser ways. Her words
summon up the misty beginnings of time and declare that
the first creative thought of God went forth in love and
delight. The circling, dancing words bring home the mystery of a world in the first air of dawn, its governing principle a child-like joy.

The Book of Job must be counted among the finest poems of
the world, while the language of Ecclesiastes, passing between poetry and melodious prose, is certainly one of the
treasures of Hebrew literature. While the theme of creation
often evokes fine poetry in the Hebrew wisdom books, tragic
themes are voiced in a poetry of outstanding passion and
beauty. Good examples of the tragic are Job's opening lament
and Qohelet's depiction of death's approach in old age:

Perish the day that I was born
and the night that said
A man is conceived! . . .
That night – let it be barren!
Let no joyful cry sound in it . . .
let the stars of its twilight be darkened!
May it long for daybreak but not see it,
nor look into the eyelids of dawn,

> because it did not shut the womb's doors on me
> and so hide misery from my eyes!
>
> Job 3.2–10

> Remember your Creator in the days of your vigour
> while the days of pain are not yet come,
> nor the years of which you will say,
> I have no pleasure in them –

So Qohelet begins his elegy of life's passing, a moving poem which serves to reinforce his call to enjoy the gift of life while we have it. The imagery leaves room for meditation and imagination, as it evokes the loss of life's colour, the failing of hands, legs, teeth and eyes, the restless nights, deafness, hoary head, bent limbs, loss of sexual desire, the last days, the preparations of the skilled mourners, the final snapping of the living cord:

> – while the sun or the light
> or the moon or the stars be not darkened,
> nor the clouds regathered after the rain,
> in the day when the keepers of the house shake
> and the strong men are bowed,
> and the grinders cease because they are few,
> and those who look out from the windows are
> darkened . . .
> and the almond tree blossoms white,
> and the grasshopper crawls wearily,
> and the caperberry proves no remedy,
> for man goes to his last home
> and the mourners gather round the street,
> till the silver cord be loosed
> and the golden bowl be broken,
> and the jar broken at the fountain
> and the pitcher broken at the well,
> and the dust falls back in the earth as it was,
> and the breath returns to God who gave it.
>
> Eccles. 12

Now and again the wisdom books express appreciation of beautiful speech:

Golden apples in silver filigree:
a speech spoken when its turn comes.

Prov. 25.11

Flowing honey: lovely sayings!
Sweet to the soul, healing to the bones!

16.24

The wise in heart shall be called discerning,
but sweetness of lips increases learning.

16.21

A wise heart makes its mouth skilled.

16.23

In the circles of the wise, they knew well that beautiful
utterance could satisfy, causing deep silence to fall upon its
hearers; and it could revive the spirit as rain comes to the
parched land. So Job recalls:

After my word they spoke no more.
My speech had dropped softly on them,
while they waited eagerly for me as for rain
and opened wide their mouth as for spring showers.

Job 29.22f.

The poetic expression of the sages, von Rad affirms, was
itself part of the perception of truth, the expression of
intensive encounter with realities; the perception exists in this
form or not at all. And he cites the ancient Greek view
represented by Pindar:

Blind is the mind of one who, without the Muses,
seeks out the steep path of wisdom.[27]

Attentiveness

For artist and contemplative a fundamental quality is attentiveness. The significance of attention is basically the same
whether the direction is to the utterly great – to God – or to
some humble thing. There is an opening of heart, a willing-
ness to receive, a quietness, a turning from self or a self-
giving. As a Taoist text puts it:

> Throw open the gates,
> put self aside,
> bide in silence,
> and the radiance of the spirit will come in
> and make its home.[28]

'Prayer consists of attention', says Simone Weil,[29] and Thomas Merton fills out the thought when he describes such prayer as the resting of mind and will upon God, turned to him and intent upon him, absorbed in his own light, a simple gaze which silently tells God that we have left everything else and desire to leave our own selves for his sake.[30]

The attention may be directed to inner depths. The Russian bishop Theophan the Recluse (1815–1894) summarized Eastern Orthodoxy's theme of attention through the 'heart' thus:

> To pray is to descend with the mind into the heart, and there to stand before the face of the Lord, ever present, all-seeing within you.[31]

The 'heart', understood as the centre of our total being, has a key role also in contemplative attention to things around us. Expounding St Augustine's teaching, Rowan Williams shows how he thought of all beauty, in some degree, as piercing our blindness and deafness, leading us away from the over-dominating, organizing life of the intellect, arousing the sense of wonder; only the heart can truly respond, as not seeking always to control but rather to enjoy.[32]

Evelyn Underhill, drawing together artist and mystic, writes of that deep knowing of a thing by an attention which unites us with it, an interpenetration of it and ourselves. It gives itself to us as we give ourselves to it. And she quotes a Sufi saying:

> Pilgrimage to the place of the wise
> is to escape the flame of separation.

Wisdom is the fruit of such communion, ignorance the portion of those who stand apart, judging, analysing what they have never truly known.[33]

Such a path of attention is thoroughly pursued in Buddhist meditation. Beyond discursive reasoning, one contemplates till the gap disappears; one dies to self, becoming one with what is contemplated, and so with the universal reality.[34]

Simone Weil's little essay has special interest for us in its linking the theme of attention with school studies. She grasps the spiritual dimension of ordinary scholastic learning in a way which prepares for our recognition of contemplation in the schooling of the ancient disciples:

> The development of the faculty of attention forms the real object and almost the sole interest of studies.

Writing of the precious gifts received more by waiting than by grasping, she sees in the solution of a geometry problem a little fragment of a particular truth and so 'a pure image of the unique, eternal and living Truth'. Because of the school's cultivation of attention, academic work is a field containing a pearl worth all our endeavour.[35]

One of the greatest English spiritual writers, William Law (1686–1761), prized attention. 'All the world preaches to an attentive mind,' he wrote, 'and if you have but ears to hear, almost everything you meet teaches you some lesson of wisdom.'[36]

In the schools of the Old Testament sages, the attentive heart was likewise greatly prized. Of all that he could have asked of the world's treasures, Solomon chose only the heart that hears (*leb shome'*):

> Give your servant a hearing heart.
>
> I Kings 3.9

Prominent in the opening chapters of Proverbs are the calls to the disciple for openness and attention: 'Hear . . . turn . . . receive . . . be attentive . . . plead for insight . . . seek . . . incline your ear . . . receive . . . keep your heart with vigilance . . . let not your heart turn aside . . . listen . . . watch . . . wait . . . !' So valuable is attention that it is thought of as fresh from the Creator's hand:

> A listening ear and a seeing eye,
> the Lord indeed has made them both.
>
> Prov. 20.12

Only from the attentive can enduring words be expected:

> A listening person speaks for eternity.
>
> 21.28

This proverb regards the opposite type of person as nothing less than 'a lying witness'.

Good deeds are the consequence of attention:

> One with a good eye shall be blessed (by the poor),
> for he gives of his own bread to the destitute.
>
> 22.9

There is a stillness and inner depth in this attention, rewarded with a Presence, and contrasting with the frantic pursuit of one-knows-not-what that finds but waste and folly:

> Before the face of the discerning person is Wisdom,
> while the eyes of the fool rove to the ends of the earth.
>
> 17.24

> The thinking of the perceptive is fruitful,
> but everyone who rushes about – it is only to lack.
>
> 21.5

Deep, deep within are the roots of attention, and deep within the teachings of wisdom are kept and enjoyed without distraction, and so nourish the whole person and come to fine expression in speech:

> Bend your ear and hear the words of the wise,
> and your heart – settle it on my knowledge,
> for the words are sweet if you keep them in your belly,
> they will be well ordered on your lips.
>
> 22.17f.

Nothing in God's creation is too slight to deserve profound attention. The sage considers till he is overcome with wonder:

> Three things I name too wonderful for me,
> yes, four beyond my knowing –
> the eagle's way in the heavens,
> the snake's way on a rock,
> a ship's way in the heart of the sea,
> and a man's way in a woman.
>
> 30.18f.

Wonder fills him too as he observes and enters the life of small and flimsy but exceedingly wise creatures: the ant, the badger, the locust, the lizard (30.24–28).

It is all akin to the wonder that opens the heart to the immediacy of God's presence in the great speeches of the Lord to Job (Job 38–41). Here the poet's observation of the heavens, the waters and the creatures of the wild is that of a loving artist. The waves and mists carry him at once to the beginning of things, when the sea burst from the womb and God confined it, swaddled it in clouds and set it in a cradle of cliffs and shores (38.8–11).

The poet has watched the dawn with wonder. He has seen the first light dart across the skies, and it seemed to him as a bright angel that lifted up the fringes of night's coverlet and shook out the marauders of darkness. And he saw how, when daylight grew from the east, lines and forms stood out in distant landscapes, as clay responds to a seal (38.12–14). Light and dark, snow, hail, rain, lightning, ice, constellations he considers with deep awe (38.16–38). He reflects on the marvels of animal life in the wilderness: the birth and feeding of the young, the free running of the wild ass, the strength of the wild ox, the migrations and high flying of the birds. To all these the poet-sage gives his attention, and thus he hears them speak to him of the mystery of creation and the Creator. In them indeed, attentive still, he meets that mystery.

Yes, the sages of old Israel listened and watched in the spirit of contemplation, and it was with a happy choice of words that Jesus ben Sira said of his own place, late in the tradition, that he was the last of those 'on watch', or 'wakeful' (Ecclus. 33.16).

Humility

Closely connected with attentiveness is humility, and likewise recognized by contemplatives to be of great importance. For the Desert Fathers, Abba Or puts it succinctly:

The crown of the monk is humility.[37]

Abba Anthony tells of the power of humility:

> I saw the snares that envy spread out over the earth,
> and I said, groaning, Who can get through such snares?
> Then I heard a voice say to me, Humility.[38]

St Augustine prizes it as corresponding to the manner of the Lord's own coming. In the journey from science to wisdom – from external knowledge to contemplation of the eternal – the soul must respond to the One who stooped in incarnation and who says:

> Humble I am come.
> I am come to teach humility
> and am come as the master of humility . . .
> he who would cleave to me must be humble.[39]

In the work ascribed to Denys, so influential in the Middle Ages, patterns of three-fold hierarchy are found everywhere on the path to God, but the aim of the devout is not to climb up rungs, but to 'ascend' inwards into deeper communion with him who has made the orders. In his will is peace, not in ambition to promote oneself.[40] Summing up the long Christian tradition on this theme, Thomas Merton points out the intrinsic connection of humility and joy:

> It is almost impossible to overestimate the value of true humility . . . if we were incapable of humility, we would be incapable of joy, because humility alone can destroy the self-centredness that makes joy impossible.[41]

Humility is a particular emphasis in Chinese Taoism, and again a correspondence is found with the nature of the ultimate power, the unconditioned, the Tao, ground of being. The great symbol of humility here is water, which runs to the lowest ground, yet there is nearest to Tao and able to overcome all:

> The best of men is like water,
> which benefits all things
> and does not compete with them;
> it dwells low in the places all disdain
> and there comes near to Tao.[42]

How did the great rivers and seas get their kingship over all the lesser streams? Through the merit of being lower than they.[43] The wise man acts, but does not appropriate; he accomplishes, but does not take the credit:

> Because he lays claim to no credit,
> the credit cannot be taken from him.[44]

Such humility, nearest to Tao, is also the secret of the 'female' principle, Yin; it accomplishes the mightiest tasks:

> In opening and shutting the gates of heaven
> can you still take the part of the Female?[45]

For the Indian Kabir, also, humility is the way to know God:

> The Presence of God
> Is like grains of sugar
> In a pile of sand;
> An elephant
> Can't pick them
> But an ant
> Knows the way!

> O Kabir, listen:
> Truth is very subtle.
> Be humble to seek it.[46]

In Old Testament wisdom we find both high praise of humility and a corresponding onslaught on arrogance. There is frequent warning not to be 'wise in one's own eyes':

> Do you see a man wise in his own eyes?
> There is more hope for a fool than for him.
>
> > Prov. 26.12

In a list of 'six things which the Lord hates, seven which are detestable to him' the first to be listed is 'eyes that are high' (6.16f.). The guiding light of the wicked, leading them astray, is their vanity and ambition: 'height of eyes and width of heart' (21.4). The most reprehensible character in Proverbs is the 'scoffer' (leṣ), and he is the most presumptuous of all:

> Arrogant, overweening? His name is Scoffer;
> he acts with upsurging arrogance.
>
> > 21.24

The success of the self-exalted is judged hollow, while humility leads to true value:

> The pride of man brings him low,
> but one lowly in spirit shall have glory.
>
> 29.23

By the path of sensitivity to God, one comes to wisdom, which is as much as to say that by the way of humility one comes to true honour:

> The fear of the Lord is the discipline leading to wisdom,
> and before glory is humility.
>
> 15.33

Without such humility under God, there is no wisdom worthy of the name:

> There is no wisdom and no understanding
> and no counsel over against the Lord.
>
> 21.30

Awareness of God continually prompted the seeker of knowledge to recognize that he was ever approaching a world that surpassed human powers of understanding. As von Rad says:

> This fear of God has trained him to openness, to readiness for an encounter with the inscrutable and the imponderable; it has taught him that the sphere in which definite, verifiable systems of order can be discerned is a very limited one.[47]

His way, then, must be in humility. And the theme is eloquently maintained by Ben Sira:

> My son, perform your tasks in humility . . .
> The greater you are,
> the more you must humble yourself . . .
> Great as is the might of the Lord,
> he is glorified by the humble . . .
> Reflect upon what has been given to you,
> for you do not need what he has hidden . . .
> already matters too great for human understanding
> have been shown to you . . .
>
> Ecclus. 3.17f.

A saying of his is echoed by Rabbi Levitas in the Sayings of the Fathers (4.4): 'Very, very lowly of spirit be!'

Love

Evelyn Underhill couples together as the supreme artistic virtues humility and love.[48] And with love we have come to the heart of the contemplative way. Love, says Dean Inge, is 'the true hierophant of the mysteries of God'.[49] And St John of the Cross gives us the shortest definition of contemplation as 'knowledge through love'.[50] In their various idioms the world's contemplatives all respond to the perception that:

> God is love
> and he who dwells in love
> dwells in God
> and God in him.
>   I John 4.16

Lao-tzu expresses the priority thus:

> I have three treasures.
> Guard them and keep them safe.
> The first is Love,
> the second is Frugality,
> the third is Never to be first in the world.[51]

Characteristic of Indian religions is the teaching of compassion towards all living beings. A striking expression comes in the Lotus of the True Law of northern Buddhism; love becomes central as the essence of enlightenment is found in one who has progressed to the verge of Nirvana, but declines to enter till all creatures are saved.[52] Of the Sufi, Ibn Arabi, it has been said that love alone was his religion.[53] The Sufis saw in love the way to God and indeed union with God.[54]

In the mediaeval schools of Jewish mystical tradition (*qabbala*), love is central. The life of loving piety (*ḥasidut*) leads on to pure love of God and vision of his glory.[55] Expounding the great classic, the Zohar, Isidore Epstein states that the efficacy of all forms of co-operation with God – study of *tora*, prayer and so on – is determined by love.[56] The emphasis is apparent also in the mystical school at Saphed in Galilee; their evening meditation included the prayer:

> Lord of the universe, I forgive all who have angered or harmed me. May no one be punished for my sake.

They apprehended the universe as a closely knit system in which all parts are sensitively dependent on each other. A deed or a thought affecting one has effect also on the whole, and love towards God must be bound up with love for every creature.[57] This is a common contemplative theme and is well expressed by Evelyn Underhill:

> Stretch out by a deliberate act of loving will towards one of the myriad manifestations of life that surround you . . . from alp to insect, anything will do, provided that your attitude be right . . . one truly apprehended will be the gateway to the rest.[58]

The Old Testament sage, as we saw in our consideration of attention, humbly contemplated 'alp and insect'. He characterized the right-living person as 'one who knows the soul of his animal', truly caring for his donkey or cattle, whereas the wicked were revealed in the cruelty of their feelings (Prov. 12.10). One fully reconciled to God need not fear wild animals, for they too share in the loving harmony (Job 5.22). Towards humans the sages would have their disciples show a love that goes beyond the exact rights of a case, a love that passes over injuries:

> Hatred insists on dispute,
> but love covers over all sins.
>
> Prov. 10.12

> A man's wisdom makes him slow to anger,
> his glory is to pass over sin done to him.
>
> 19.11

> By steadfast love and truth iniquity is forgiven,
> and by fear of the Lord there is avoidance of evil.
>
> 16.6

There is no tit-for-tat in the life of love. If you have been falsely represented, do not repay:

> Do not be a wanton witness against your neighbour
> and do not mislead with your lips.
> Do not say, As he has done to me,
> so I will do to him,
> I will pay the man back according to his deed.
>
> 24.28f.

More positively, one should requite enmity with kindness:

> If he who hates you is hungry, give him bread to eat,
> if he is thirsty, give him water to drink,
> for thus you will heap coals (of repentance) on his head
> and the Lord in turn will requite you.
>
> 25.21f.

Not even in your heart should you take satisfaction in an adversary's misfortune:

> One who scorns a poor man
> derides his maker.
> One who rejoices at another's calamity
> will not be acquitted.
>
> 17.5

> When your enemy falls
> do not rejoice,
> when he stumbles
> let not your heart exult,
> lest the Lord see
> and it displease him
> and he deflect his anger from him (to you).
>
> 24.17f.

In the same spirit Job solemnly swears that he has not rejoiced at the ruin of one who hated him, or exulted when harm befell him (Job 31.29).

The sages value the unchanging love of a true friend and the brotherly love which is there to help in the hour of need (Prov. 17.17). It is the Lord we meet in the needy person:

> Whoever is generous to a poor man
> lends to the Lord –
> he will amply repay him.
>
> 19.17; cf. 14.31

The expression 'to love God' is not characteristic of the wisdom books, though found in Ecclesiasticus (1.10 etc.). The perfect relation to God is typically described as 'fearing God', as in the model case of Job: 'There is none to compare with him in the earth, a man complete and straight, fearing God and departing from evil' (Job 1.8). The language of love is,

however, used for the response to God's approach in the
mysterious person of Wisdom. The disciple is urged:

> Do not forsake her and she will keep you,
> love her and she will guard you.
>
> Prov. 4.6

Such love she returns:

> Those who love me do I love,
> and those who seek me eagerly shall find me.
>
> 8.17

She speaks blessing on the one who listens, waits and watches
at her doors (8.34).

Passionate love of Wisdom is taught by Ben Sira:

> Whoever loves her loves life,
> and those who rise early to seek her
> will be filled with joy,
> and holding her fast
> will obtain glory.
>
> Ecclus. 4.12f.

> Stalk her like a hunter
> and lie in wait on her paths.
> Whoever peers through her windows
> and listens at her door,
> camping beside her house,
> fixing his tent-peg in her wall . . .
> will be sheltered by her from the heat
> and dwell in the midst of her glory . . .
> She will come to meet him like a mother
> and welcome him like a young bride.
>
> 14.22f.

And as Proverbs ends with an acrostic poem on the ideal wife,
Ben Sira concludes his work with one on the love of Wisdom.
It is a story of devoted love, which is not disappointed:

> While still young and untravelled,
> I sought openly for Wisdom in my prayers.
> Before the temple I asked for her
> and I will seek her out to the end.
> From blossom to ripening grape
> my heart has delighted in her . . .

> I directed my soul towards her
> and by the way of purity I found her.
>
> 51.13f.

About a century after Ben Sira, the author of The Wisdom of Solomon, sometimes influenced by Greek thought, maintains the tradition. He represents Solomon asking God for Wisdom with especial warmth:

> I loved her and sought her when I was young
> and longed to take her for my bride
> and fell in love with her beauty . . .
> So I determined to take her to live with me,
> knowing she would counsel me in prosperity
> and comfort me in cares and sorrow . . .
> When I come home I find peace with her,
> for in her company is no bitterness
> and life with her has no pain,
> but is delight and joy.
>
> Wisdom 8.2f.

This author expressed well the essence of the long tradition of romance with Wisdom: they love and long for her because 'she makes them friends of God' (7.27).

Here, then, we can recognize a particular love that is directed to God. But as we have seen, the life of wisdom was in general a life of caring and showing good-will and forbearance. It is especially the steady, constant, faithful love which the sages valued:

> Faithful love and truth – never let them go,
> bind them on your throat,
> write them on the tablet of your heart.
>
> Prov. 3.3

Limits of understanding

It is characteristic of the contemplative way to respect the limits of what we can say of God: to acknowledge the hiddenness, the inexpressible otherness, the mystery, the 'negative way' in which it may be better to speak of what God is not.

Several decades before the New Testament's Paul and John, Philo of Alexandria lived in a confluence of Greek and Hebrew wisdom. He was emphatic that God in his essence remained beyond man's knowing, utterly transcendent. The highest level of God's self-disclosure was that of his Logos – his Thought and Word:

> Do not suppose that the Existent, which truly exists, is apprehended by any man . . . Not even a proper name can be given to the truly Existent . . . Do not, then, be thoroughly perplexed if you find the highest of all beings to be ineffable, when his Logos, too, cannot be expressed by us through his own name. And indeed, if he is ineffable, he is also inconceivable and incomprehensible.[59]

A great exponent of the negative way was the fifth-century Denys. He describes how the mind drawn towards God ascends beyond concepts, images and thoughts to an area of darkness. There is a blacking out of conceptual knowledge, but the inner eye is filled with light. It is a going to God through unknowing.[60]

There are many illustrations of a similar realization of the limits of conceptual knowledge in the far east. From the Chinese Taoists we have several poems on the mystery:

> The Tao that can be told of
>   is not the absolute Tao,
> the names that can be given
>   are not the absolute names.
>
> Looked at, but cannot be seen –
>   that is called the Invisible;
> listened to, but cannot be heard –
>   that is called the Inaudible;
> grasped for, but cannot be touched –
>   that is called the Intangible.
> These three elude all our enquiries
> and hence blend and become One . . .
>   the Form of the Formless,
>   the Image of Nothingness . . .
>   the Elusive.[61]

From the meeting of Taoism and Buddhism came the great meditative practice of Zen. Here again the limits of thought and logical explanation are keenly recognized and intuition cultivated. Teaching was passed on with avoidance of formal statement.[62]

The Taoist sages greatly valued one who had attained to knowledge of his ignorance:

> Whoever knows that he does not know is highest;
> sick of mind is one who pretends to know what
>   he does not know.[63]

A saying of Confucius makes the same point:

> To know what you know
> and know what you do not know
> is the mark of one who knows.[64]

We have already noticed the story from the Egyptian Desert Fathers where the spiritual director praised the answer of Abba Joseph: he had found the way for he had said, 'I do not know.' Another story from these Fathers shows how we have to acknowledge inexplicable mysteries:

> When Abba Anthony thought about the depths of the judgments of God he asked, Lord . . . . why do the wicked prosper and why are the just in need? He heard a voice answering him, Anthony, keep your attention on yourself. These things are according to the judgment of God, and it is not to your advantage to know anything about them.[65]

Von Rad has called the Israelite wisdom teachers 'hymnists of the divine mysteries',[66] and he thinks their teaching about the limits of understanding affords the best standpoint for viewing their whole undertaking.[67] He connects with this the absence of systems in their teaching. They offer no ambitious construction for understanding the world, but only intuitive flashes and poetic fragments. Only in this way could they perceive order in a world that must remain entirely open to God.[68] It was not an inability to think, but an insight into the limits of human control. They were aware that:

> the truth about the world and man can never become the object of our theoretical knowledge; that reliable knowledge

can only be achieved through a relation of trust with things; that it is the highest wisdom to abstain from the attempt to control wisdom in abstract terms; that it is much wiser to let things retain their constantly puzzling nature, and that means to allow them to become themselves active, and by what they have to say, to set men to rights.[69]

In Proverbs the theme of limits to understanding takes various forms. There are a number of sayings which note how the best laid plans of man crumble before the mysterious decisions of God, for example:

Many are the reckonings in the human heart,
but the counsel of the Lord – that is what will stand.
                              Prov. 19.21; cf. 16.1f.

From the Lord are the steps of a person,
then man – how shall he understand his way?
                              20.24

Kings need to be well-informed about matters in their realm, but over and around the busy human stage is mysterious darkness:

To conceal a thing – this is the glory of God.
To search things out – this is the glory of kings.
                              25.2

It is no doubt true of idealistic movements that they stand in danger of betraying their own ideals. Poor monks grow into rich establishments, communists become privileged tyrants, and humble scholars become intellectually vain. Not only from prophets like Isaiah and Jeremiah, but also from the wisdom teachings themselves we have evidence of reaction against such betrayal. The apparently obscure beginning to the utterance of Agur (Prov. 30.1) may be explained as using allegorical names rather in the manner of John Bunyan and the sense would then be: 'The utterance of a mortal man to Mr I-am-God, to Mr I-am-God-and-I-can do-it.' The message then proceeds with ironic humility:

Yes, I am more brute than man
and have not human understanding,
and I have not learned wisdom,
nor known the knowledge of things divine.

Who has gone up to heaven and come down again?
Who has gathered the wind in his fists?
Who has wrapped the waters in his garment?
Who has set the bounds of the earth?
What was his name, and the name of his son?
Doubtless you will know!

30.2f.

The passage resembles the Lord's speech in Job, which conveys an immediate impression of the greatness of God beyond all human argument:

Where were you when I founded the earth?
Explain it, if you have understanding.
Who determined its measurements – surely you know –
or who stretched the line across it?
On what were its bases sunk,
or who laid its corner-stone,
when the morning stars sang together
and all the sons of God shouted praise?

38.4–7

One may say that the whole drama of Job is directed against the explainers, the ones who seem to control God in their systems of thought. The artist conveys confidentially to his audience that heaven has its reasons for Job's calamity, but to the drama's end Job is never given an explanation. It is interesting also that though Job's counsellors are in the end found guilty of presumption, and though Job himself only near the end receives the full impact of the divine mystery, yet all parties have had eloquent things to say on our theme. It was obviously a subject commonly treated among the wise. So Job exclaims:

He does great things beyond understanding,
marvellous things without number.
Look, he passes by me, and I do not see him,
he moves one, but I do not perceive him . . .
Who can say to him, What are you doing?

9.10f.

The third friend, Zophar, asks ironically:

> Can you find out the deep things of God?
> Can you find out the limit of the Almighty?
> It is higher than heaven – what can you do?
> deeper than the Netherworld – what can you know?
>
> > 11.7f.

Later, a fine statement of the theme is ascribed to Job:

> Before God the Underworld is naked,
> the Land of the Perished uncovered.
> He stretches out the sky-vault over the void
> and hangs the earth on nothing . . .
> See, these are but the fringes of his ways,
> and how small a whisper do we hear of him!
> Then who could understand the thunder of his power?
>
> > 26.6f.

Our theme has, further, what seems to be an independent poem devoted to it, preserved in chapter 28. Here the technology of mining illustrates man's skill in searching out and acquiring remote and hidden things like precious metals and stones. The poet pictures the silver mines, the gold refining, the shafts driven deep into subterranean darkness to take iron and copper from earth and stone. In remote valleys miners hang far beneath the feet of travellers. Flint and mountain side give way as the miners cleave channels to reach every precious stone. Even from the sources of rivers they bring up hidden treasure. But when it comes to the divine Wisdom, man is powerless. The thought and plan and skill and power of God in creating and sustaining the living universe – here is a mystery which must ever elude creature-man. Only God himself beholds and knows her, attendant as she is in all his work of creation. She is the ultimate depth of beauty and truth in creation, open to God alone, beyond man's grasp and mastery. For man there remains a humble way: his best wisdom is to fear God and shun evil.

Even Elihu, the rather brash youth, chimes in:

> God is greater than we can know . . .
> The Almighty – we cannot find him.
>
> > 36.26; 37.23

Thus all the speakers in the drama can hold forth on this theme.
It is not a new doctrine only disclosed at the grand resolution,
when the Lord speaks from the tempest (38.1f.). The drama
illustrates the fact that there is all the difference in the world
between knowing something with the head and knowing it
with the heart – knowing about something and knowing it
directly. The drama indeed has a movement and a climax. To
echo phrases of Martin Buber, 'all means collapse' and then
'true meeting comes about'.[70] This unattainable, transcendent
God is filling Job's heaven and all else lives in his light:

> I had heard of you only by hear-say,
> but now my own eyes see you.
>
> 42.5

The later Hebrew sages sustain the theme. Qohelet senses
the immense mystery of God and severe limits for human
enquiry:

> I said, I will become wise,
> but that was far beyond me.
> Far is what is,
> deep, so deep – who can find it?
>
> Eccles. 7.23f.

> I considered all the work of God,
> that man is unable to find out all the work . . .
> and even if the wise man says he knows,
> he is not able to find it out.
>
> 8.17

In the school of Ben Sira the lesson was often repeated:

> Do not meddle with matters beyond your tasks.
> Even what has been assigned to you is beyond
>   human understanding.
>
> Ecclus. 3.23

> To none has he given power to tell all the story of his
>   works,
> and who can fathom his marvellous acts? . . .
> No one can diminish or increase them
> or track down the wonders of the Lord.
> Get to the end of them and you are just beginning,
> finish, and you are baffled still.
>
> 18.4f.

In face of the wonders of God, words of praise were indeed appropriate, but these too must fall short:

> Look at the rainbow and praise him who made it . . .
> However much we speak, we cannot reach the end,
> and the sum of our words is – he is all . . .
> Who has seen him and can describe him,
> who can praise him as he is?
> Many things greater than these stay hidden
> and we have seen but a little of his works.
>
> 43.11–32

Silence

From limits of knowledge we can pass readily to considerations of silence and restraint of speech. Contemplatives of east and west would appreciate Qohelet's saying:

> God is in heaven and you are on earth,
> therefore let your words be few.
>
> Eccles. 5.2

The epilogue to his book even extends the advice to written words – a little is enough:

> The multiplication of books is endless,
> and the study of them yields only exhaustion.
>
> 12.12

Ancient Egyptian wisdom constantly teaches the value of silence and slowness to speak:

> The innermost chamber opens to the man of silence.
> Do not talk much; be silent and you will be happy . . .[71]

> The dwelling of God – its abomination is clamour.
> Pray with a loving heart, all its words being hidden,
> and he will do what you need.[72]

The inappropriateness and inadequacy of words, spoken or written, in the deeper contacts with truth were keenly felt by the Chinese Taoists. Books could be regarded as the discarded husk or shell of wisdom, while words themselves, being from superficial levels of experience, could not suffice for deeper knowledge.[73] The Tao could only be mirrored in a still pool.[74] Lao-tzu says:

> He who knows does not speak,
> he who speaks does not know.[75]

Confucius also valued such reticence. He said, 'I would prefer not to speak.' His disciples answered, 'If our master did not speak, what would your little ones have to hand down about him?' To this Confucius replied, 'What does Heaven say? Yet the four seasons run their course and the hundred creatures are born through it.' The cosmic order functions without words, and the wise person emulates the silent ways of Heaven.[76]

The 'negative way' of Denys, mentioned in our previous section, leads at last to silence. When all concepts have been denied, the soul becomes completely speechless in union with the Inexpressible.[77] Whether in such mystical depths, or in the general life of humility and attention, the fitness of silence and economy of speech is generally accepted by contemplatives. In Christian monastic life there is much regulation of silent periods, and the stories of the Desert Fathers show how the ideal was present in the early days. Abba Arsenius, for example, declared that he had often repented of having spoken, but never of having been silent.[78] Of Abba Or it was said that he never lied, never swore, nor hurt anyone, nor spoke without necessity.[79] In the world of Islam we hear of a Sufi master who said of a man who was studying grammar, 'It would be better for him if he studied silence.'[80] In modern India Mahatma Ghandi in his ashram always maintained one day of total silence each week.

Economy of speech was much valued by the Old Testament sages. The wise are pictured as knowing when silence is best and as reflecting before answering. The fools, on the other hand, speak much, speak readily, and thereby cause much harm:

> The sages store up knowledge,
> but the mouth of a fool is imminent disaster.
>
> Prov. 10.14

> In a mass of words sin will not be lacking,
> but a wise man restrains his lips.
>
> 10.19

One lacking heart pours scorn on his fellow,
but a man of understanding keeps silent.

11.12

The gossip reveals intimate conversation,
but the trusty in spirit conceals the confidence.

11.13

The perceptive man covers knowledge,
but the heart of fools proclaims folly.

12.23

The heart of a righteous person meditates what to answer,
but the mouth of the wicked pours out evil.

15.28

Even a fool, when silent, may be thought wise;
sealing his lips, he may seem discerning.

17.28

The sage found the example of God instructive (30.6): when God speaks, he speaks true, his word like pure metal from the refiner. Anyone receiving such a rare word of revelation can trust him. Let not man multiply words beyond God's, for the human unreliability will soon become apparent.

For Qohelet it is man's situation in the midst of infinite mystery that makes much talking inappropriate. Why should he hold forth as if he held his destiny in his own hands?

> Whatever comes to pass,
> already its name has been given,
> and it is known what man is,
> and he is not able to dispute
> with one that is stronger than he,
> for the more words, the more vanity.
> What does it profit man?
>
> Eccles. 6.10f.

> A stupid person speaks many words –
> man knows not what shall be,
> and who can tell him
> what will be after him?
>
> 10.14

Ben Sira advised his disciples to be 'quick to hear, deliberate in answering' (Ecclus. 5.11). Words should be weighed, and the mouth sometimes firmly shut:

> Make balances and scales for your words,
> and a door and bolt for your mouth.
>
> 28.25f.

The young person in society is especially advised to speak only if there is need, and then as briefly as possible:

> Speak, young man, if you are needed,
> but twice at the most, and only if asked.
> Be brief, say much in few words.
> Be as one who knows, and yet keeps silent.
>
> 32.7f.

The wise man keeps silent till he knows the right moment to speak has come. He is careful not to exceed the moment, which is the failing of braggarts and fools (20.6f.).

The ideal continued into the circles of the rabbis, as appears in a saying of Simeon preserved in The Sayings of the Fathers (1.7):

> All my days I have grown up among the wise, and I
> have not found anything better for one than silence.

Life as given

Contemplatives see everywhere the priority of God who has surrounded us with his appointments and gifts. Life itself is a gift, and every aspect is full of the divine initiative. Anthony Bloom speaks for the long tradition of the eastern church in his foreword to the Sayings of the Desert Fathers and emphasizes the sense of gift:

> Modern man mainly seeks for 'experience' – putting himself at the centre of things, he wishes to make them subservient to this aim . . . Such an attitude the Desert Fathers repudiated as sacrilegious: the experiential knowledge which God in his infinite love and condescension gives to those who seek him with their whole heart is always a gift; its essential abiding quality is its gratuity.[81]

Thomas Merton also stresses the 'givenness' of the fruits of contemplation:

> In contemplation . . . everything is yours; but on one infinitely important condition – that it is all *given*. There is nothing that you can claim, nothing that you can demand, nothing that you can *take* . . . we must realize to the very depths of our being that this is a pure gift of God which no desire, no effort and no heroism of ours can do anything to deserve or obtain.[82]

Whatever the discipline and application needed for the pilgrim's way, he can make no claim for it all, but only receive the gift.

The Chinese sages were particularly sensitive to this side of contemplative experience. Confucius describes the wise man as 'quiet and calm, waiting for the appointments of Heaven'.[83] He counsels:

> Resign yourself to the sequence of things,
> not brooding over the changes of life,
> and you enter into the pure, the divine, the One.[84]

In Birmingham's General Hospital there is a fish-tank in a waiting room, intended no doubt to be calming to the spirit. Confucius would love it, for it was a favourite image of the life of grace:

> Fish are happy in water,
> man in Tao.[85]

The wise person, Lao-tzu noted, loved choosing the right time for his actions.[86] It was not a question of shrewd judgment, but of being open and patient towards what was given. Facing suffering and death, a sage would accept the appointments of each time with contentment:

> This is to be freed from bondage . . .
> I obtained life because it was my time,
> and I am now parting with it in accordance with Tao.

> Content with the coming of things in their time,
> and living in accordance with Tao,
> joy and sorrow touch me not.[87]

As a child accepts the present time, so simply must even great men live, keeping the warm heart of a child. Mencius (372–289 BC) defined our moral problem as how to keep 'that air of the early dawn through the day'.[88] Yang Chu (fourth century BC) deplored ambition and sophistication:

> We waste ourselves in a mad scramble,
> seeking to snatch the hollow praise of an hour . . .
> We move through the world in a narrow groove,
> preoccupied with the petty things we see and hear,
> brooding over our prejudices,
> passing by the joys of life,
> without ever knowing that we have missed anything.[89]

The greatest challenge to contentment, death itself, was faced by these sages with tranquillity. Birth and death could not increase or diminish the sum of all existence. Joined with the movement of the primitive reality, Tao, dying itself was a joy. In Tao was simplicity, calm and contentment.[90]

Kabir sang of respect for the given times:

> Wait for
> The opportune moment,
> O my heart.
> Everything happens
> At its own pace!
> The gardener may flood
> The orchard with water,
> But the trees
> Don't bear fruit
> Out of season.[91]

The teaching was already familiar to the ancient Egyptians:

> It is God who assigns the foremost place,
> one attains nothing with the elbow.[92]

> Do not be miserly with your wealth
> which has accrued to you as a gift of God.[93]

When we turn to the Israelite sages, we find a deep sense of God's appointments and gifts on every hand. Disciplined and dedicated as was the way they taught, the prize of Wisdom was not to be seized by human effort or ability. According to

Proverbs (1.20f.; 8.1f.), she came even to the busy, heedless throng, offering to pour out her spirit and words of life. The disciple is urged to incline his attention and heart to her, to cry out for her, and seek her as the greatest treasure, but in the end he 'finds' what God has prepared, he receives a gift:

> It is the Lord who gives wisdom,
> from his mouth come knowledge and understanding.
>
> Prov. 2.1f.

Happy the one who finds Wisdom, a bountiful figure, her two hands laden with gifts (3.13f.)!

Work is commended, as we shall see, but its yield is ascribed to the fructifying touch of God's grace, rather than to the intensity of human effort:

> It is the blessing of the Lord that enriches,
> and anxious toil can add nothing to it.
>
> 10.22

The appointments of God gave the sages the sense that he made everything for its own purpose, for 'what answered to it', and the thought was applied ironically to the puzzling existence of the wicked:

> Everything has the Lord made for its proper end,
> and even the wicked man for the day of calamity.
>
> 16.4

The wise man knew that in every endeavour he was looking to find the good which the Lord had prepared; his work was done with a sense of trust in the all-embracing, creating hands of God:

> One wisely undertaking a matter will find good,
> and trusting in the Lord, how blessed he shall be!
>
> 16.20

Needless to say, the generous God who was there ahead of you was acknowledged in so great a matter as marriage; here indeed was a gift to find:

> Has he found a wife? He has found good
> and obtained grace from the Lord.
>
> 18.22

> House and wealth you may inherit from your fathers,
>   but a wise woman you receive from the Lord.
>
> 19.14

Again and again Qohelet refers to the gifts and appointments of God. This indeed is the theme which is the light in his darkness. In a famous passage of deceptive simplicity, events and activities of human life are set out in contrasting pairs, and each is said to have its appointed time. It becomes clear from the chapter as a whole that these appointments are fundamentally from God. Human wisdom then lies in recognizing our limitations in shaping our experience. Hard times and happy times can be expected in our lot, and in the midst of one we should not ignore the other:

> For everything there is an appointed moment,
> a time for every business under heaven,
> a time for birth and a time for death,
> a time to plant and a time to uproot what was planted,
> a time of killing and a time of healing,
> a time of breaking down and a time of rebuilding,
> a time to weep and a time to laugh,
> a time to mourn and a time to dance . . .
> a time of war and a time of peace.
>
> 3.1–8

Meditating further on his poem of alternating times, Qohelet affirms that God has made everything beautiful in its time. But its time under the sun is not for ever and we, who have been given by God a feeling for eternity, could well break our hearts over the fading of such beauty. But we must rest in the acceptance of his appointments and know that he cares: he himself seeks what is driven away (3.15). The 'eternity' he has given in our hearts is a great range of memory and hope, history and vision of the future, but it falls short of knowing the work of God from beginning to end. Our imagination and aspirations, then, had best be exercised in humility. Our peace will be in acceptance that the times are from him.

To eat and drink and enjoy our work – this is 'from the hand of God' (2.24–25). To rejoice and do good and see fruit in our work – 'this is the gift of God' (3.10–13).

Look, I have seen for myself what is good –
that it is beautiful for someone to eat and drink
and see good from all the toil that he toils with under
   the sun
for the number of the days of his life which God gives him,
for that is his allotted portion . . .
this is the gift of God.

5.18f.

When you eat and drink in gladness, dress cheerfully in white, and see life with your beloved spouse, you may be assured that God has already given his approval, for it is all prepared and given by him (9.7–9).

It is 'a wise heart' that knows 'the due time and appointment' (8.5–6), and so moves in harmony with God. But Qohelet recognizes that so often mankind acts against the 'time', and disorder ensues. The prizes go to the wrong hands, the wise go hungry, and people are snatched up like fish in a net or birds in a cage-trap (9.11–12).

Ben Sira puts his weight on the positive side:

All that the Lord has made is very good,
all that he commands will be done in his time.
No one can say, What is this? Why that?
for in God's time all things will be sought out.

39.16f.

He will supply every need in its time,
and no one can say, This is less good than that,
for all things will prove good in their time.

39.33f.

Such teaching of the goodness of all things in their time is not arrived at easily. It would be foolish to ascribe it to complacency. At a superficial level it seems absurd and could bring no credit to the teacher and circle that propagated it. It has to be reckoned rather among the insights which are given to contemplatives, those who, long 'on watch', see through the veil – enough to have assurance of God's all-embracing order. Ben Sira's assurance that all things are from his hand and in his hand and have their appointed time of fruition is not unlike the visionary perception of the fourteenth century mystic Julian of Norwich. Against all evidence she knew that 'all manner of thing shall be well'.[94] These are the encounters of which Martin Buber writes:

> There are moments of silent depth
> in which you look on the world-order fully present . . .
> These moments are immortal
> and most transitory of all . . .
> their power invades creation and the knowledge of man,
> beams of their power stream into the world as we usually
>   perceive it,
> and dissolve it again and again.[95]

The dark night of honesty

The image of the 'dark night' is especially that of the Spanish St John of the Cross. In drawing to God, one renounces the light of all lesser things and endures a period of great darkness of sense and spirit. Attachments to the lesser things are like cords that hold down a bird – even the slenderest must be broken if the bird is to fly.[96] There is resemblance here to the Buddhist 'nirvana' which denotes a blowing out of inferior lights of attachment or desire in readiness for the perfect illumination.[97]

In Taoism the way to inner truth and peace is challengingly expressed as the rejection of wisdom and knowledge and the return to primal simplicity. It is as though a Hebrew would undo the eating of the fruit of Eden's tree of knowledge:

> Banish wisdom, discard knowledge,
> and the people will be benefited a hundred-fold.
> Give them simplicity to contemplate,
> the uncarved block to hold,
> selflessness and fewness of desires.[98]

The marred and self-defeating nature of much human activity is keenly felt, not least in the pretensions of learning:

> Learning consists in adding to one's stock day by day,
> the practice of Tao in subtracting day by day,
> subtracting and again subtracting,
> till one has reached inactivity,
> and by this very inactivity
> everything can be activated.[99]

Here the world is seen with honest and penetrating eye, and the good way is found out amid painful recognition of much vanity:

> To labour away one's whole life-time
> but never see the result,
> to be utterly worn out with toil
> but have no idea where it leads,
> is not this lamentable?[100]

The Indian singer Kabir is another who does not fail to see life's tragedies honestly:

> Sorrow resides
> In the hearts
> Of all beings,
> O Kabir
> Such is the essence
> Of life!
>
> Between the two slabs
> Of the grindstone,
> All grains are crushed,
> There is none
> That remains
> Unscathed![101]

In east and west alike, the unmasking and discarding of illusions is found to be necessary on the path to truth. The rejection of deluding comforts, even the comforts of religion, is a harsh experience, a darkness of sense and soul, but an essential prerequisite to the enjoyment of the true light. Writing of those who enter the dark region of this 'unillusion-ment', Ruth Burrows says that there they are aware that they are more in the truth, closer to reality and so to God: 'They prefer to feel the utter emptiness of everything, the desolation and futility of life, rather than be fed what is not him.' They suffer 'the pain of honesty'.[102] Without such suffering, according to Kabir, no one can hope to see the face of the Beloved, who is king of the night of anguish.[103]

There is much in Hebrew wisdom relevant to this theme. Already in Proverbs the shadow of this night of honesty is falling. There are no illusions about much of the commisera-tion and congratulation so readily handed out in society:

> Every heart knows its own bitterness
> and no other shares its joy.
>
> Prov. 14.10

The sage's honest ear catches the drone-note of sorrow sustained under the happy songs:

> Even when laughing the heart has pain,
> and for rejoicing the end is sorrow.
>
> 14.13

He notices how we devote ourselves to fleeting goods as though they would last for ever:

> Do not labour to get rich,
> be sensible and desist.
> You take your eye off it –
> it has vanished!
> It makes itself wings,
> like an eagle it soars to the sky.
>
> 23.4f.

Can we not say of Job that he goes deep into the dark night 'rather than be fed what is not God'? His friends offer him 'the comforts of religion': if he will admit his sins as the cause of his misfortunes, acknowledging the justice of his sufferings as retribution, he will gain relief and restoration of health and honour. One after another, again and again, they earnestly plead and remonstrate with him to this effect. When he rejects their counsel and their imputations of secret wrong-doings, they accuse him of 'doing away with the fear of God and hindering meditation before him' (Job 15.4). Thus, to maintain his stand, Job must suffer the alienation from his few remaining friends to add to the apparent alienation from God.

But he will not settle for what is not true, what is therefore not God. He looks at his sufferings honestly; they have all the appearance of an unjust assault. He speaks his horror that the one who created him and led him through life with every appearance of love should all the while have intended such cruelties against him. He looks at society with honest eyes: everywhere he sees oppression of the poor and the prosperity of the oppressors:

> From out of the cities the dying victims groan
> and the souls of the wounded cry aloud for help,
> yet God pays no attention to their prayers.
>
> 24.12

But Job is not just giving vent to bitterness. Amid all the dark loneliness which his stand entails, he is set firmly in quest of God. The sum of all his speeches, shocking as they are to his pious friends, is a great call to God. He never lets go his faith in truth:

> He breaks me with breach upon breach,
> running to attack me like a warrior,
> though no violence stains my hands
> and my prayer is sincere.
> Earth, do not cover my blood
> and never let my cry be buried!
>
> Yet even now my witness is in heaven,
> he who will testify for me is on high.
> While my earthly friends abuse me,
> to God my eye is weeping . . .
>
> 16.14–20

Yes, Job suffers because he will have nothing less than God. His quest takes him beyond his material losses and torments, into the darkest night of the soul, utterly alone. Then, at last, God comes to his faithful servant, and Job sees him with his own eyes, on his side, estranged no more (19.27; 42.5).

Qohelet also was one who preferred 'to feel the utter emptiness of everything and the desolation and futility of life, rather than be fed what is not him'. He sees and fully expresses the fleeting, vaporous quality of man's endeavours: 'vanity of vanities, all is vanity' (Eccles. 1.2). Words grow weary to express the vast cycle of the world (1.8). And a sorry occupation God has given man to be occupied with – all fleeting, a shepherding of the winds (1.13–14). Man's crimes of oppression are so grievous that it would have been better to be dead, better still not to have been born, and so not to have seen the evil done under the sun (4.1–3).

But again, the book is not dedicated to the expression of bitterness or disgust. In the darkness of honesty, the lights of easy comfort extinguished, Qohelet is open to true illumination, and he declares 'the light is sweet' (11.7). It was not given him to pass beyond his darkness, but still within it he enjoys gleams of inner light. He affirms a joy for humanity in humble acceptance of God's gift, and he finds rest in the assurance that behind the fleeting surface of things is God's eternal work: 'nothing can be added to it nor taken from it . . . and God seeks what is driven away' (3.14–15) – what seems lost is not lost to him.

Early Christian contemplatives valued Qohelet very much in these terms. One of the greatest, Origen (c. 185–254), understood the three stages of the mystical life – the path to fulfilment of union with Christ – as corresponding to the three books ascribed to Solomon. Proverbs gave directions for pure living, Ecclesiastes led the soul to recognize the 'vanity' of the outward world and so prepared for the third stage, the union of love with God expressed allegorically by the Song of Songs.[104]

In the Old Testament generally there is rich material born in the sufferings which afflict peoples and individuals: vivid narratives, passionate prayers and thanksgivings, messages and interpretations of prophets. But the wisdom books have their own contribution to make. The encounter with suffering is that which comes in honest contemplation, looking at things bravely and openly, satisfied with nothing but the truth, and so ready for God.

Work

'The Lord walks among the pots and pans,' wrote St Teresa of Avila.[105] Christian contemplatives have indeed set much store on work. Released from the strains of ambition, greed and anxiety, they can enjoy work as a harmony with the Creator's work and as an expression of love. And so it is that visitors to convents are often as much moved by the spirit of the monks or nuns at work as they are by their devotions in chapel. In earlier times the Desert Fathers, in solitude in the harsh conditions of the Nitrian desert, worked regularly at the weaving of reed baskets. Abba Isaiah taught his disciples that 'whoever has not worked will not receive a reward from God'.[106]

In his famous first sermon, the Buddha set out the way to salvation in eight stages or aspects. Before the last two, which are in effect degrees of contemplation, come 'right livelihood' and 'right effort'. The 'livelihood' refers to a trade or occupation, which should be agreeable to the ideals of the 'Noble Way'. The 'effort' refers to the need for hard work and responsible use of energies.[107]

One of the most attractive of the ancient Indian texts, the Bhagavad Gita, also prizes work and action, *karma*, on the path of wisdom and salvation. Juan Mascaro, in the preface to his translation of the Gita, writes thus of *karma*:

> . . . every little finite action should be a surrender to the Infinite, even as breathing in seems to be the receiving of the gift of life, and the breathing out a surrender into the infinite Life. Every little work in life, however humble, can become an act of creation, and therefore a means of salvation, because in all true creation we reconcile the finite with the Infinite, hence the joy of creation.[108]

All work can be beautiful and holy. The Lord (Krishna) says:

> Offer to me all your works
> and rest your mind on the Supreme.
> Be free from vain hopes and selfish thoughts
> and with inner peace fight your fight.
>
> Gita 3.30[109]

Work and the contemplative stance intermingle in these counsels of Krishna:

> I will teach you the truth of pure work
> and this truth will make you free . . .
> Know also of a work that is silence –
> mysterious is the path of work.
> The man who in his work finds silence
> and who sees that silence is work,
> this man in truth sees the light
> and in all his works finds peace.
> He whose undertakings are free
> from anxious desire and fanciful thought,
> whose work is made pure in the fire of wisdom,
> he is called wise by those who see.

In whatever work he does,
such a man in truth has peace,
he expects nothing, he relies on nothing,
and ever has fullness of joy . . .
He is glad with whatever God gives him,
he has risen beyond the two contraries here below:
he is without jealousy
and in success or in failure he is one –
his works bind him not . . .
he has found peace in wisdom
and his work is a holy sacrifice.
Who in all his work sees God,
in truth goes unto God.
God is his worship,
God is his offering
offered by God
in the fire of God.

4.16–24[110]

In all this we see how within a piety of detachment, of recognition of 'vanity' in the outer world, there can exist also the highest valuation of work and activity in the world. It is work infused with the wisdom of contemplation, work in joy before the One whose own work forms and moves the universe.

What work might fall to the lot of the disciples of the Old Testament sages? There was the work of study: the arts of reading, writing, numbers, natural lore of skies and land, learning of texts and oral tradition, discussion and meditation. There was the work to which many graduated in the field of government. There was the arduous work, often under a hot sun, with the family holdings of land, trees and animals. There would be other crafts and occupations. Whatever work it was, the sages valued it as part of wisdom and done in the sight of God. To contemplate the industrious ant would not only teach one the value of work, but help one to become wise:

You idler, go to the ant!
See her ways and become wise . . .

Prov. 6.6–11

There was no question of work in the market being outside the pale. If the raw motives of self-interest were especially virulent

in the arena of trade and barter, there was all the more reason
to point to God's presence and his will for truth and fairness.
The just trader was the servant of God, handling God's scales
and weights:

> Just balances and scales belong to the Lord,
> all the weights in the bag are his work.
>
> 16.11

> Tricks with false weights and measures
> are hateful to the Lord.
>
> 20.10

There are many condemnations of idleness in work, often
with a humorous portrayal of the idler. He turns on his bed
like a door on its hinges (26.14) – long habit has rooted him to
the spot. He suffers from the constant and convenient illusion
that there is a lion outside (26.13), or so you would think; a
case not so much of agoraphobia, fear of the market-place, as
of ergophobia, a morbid dislike of work. Sitting in the circle
round the communal dish of food, he makes the effort to reach
his hand to it, but is then too fatigued to bring the food back to
his mouth (26.15). Entrusted with a mission, the work-shy
civil servant hurts those who sent him like vinegar on
sensitive teeth or smoke in the eyes (10.26).

We are advised to tackle the hard, fundamental work before
looking for enjoyment:

> First put right your work outside
> and make things ready on the land –
> after that build your house.
>
> 24.27

We are warned against the guile of self-indulgence, which
starts with 'I'll just have a little . . . a little won't do me any
harm'. The lesson is expressed as a story of personal experience:

> By the field of an idler I chanced to pass,
> by the vineyard of a man lacking heart,
> and look, it had grown a forest of thistles,
> its face was covered with weeds,
> and its wall of stones was in ruins.

I looked and I contemplated,
I saw and I learnt the lesson:
a little sleep, just a little nap,
a little folding of the hands for reclining,
and your poverty comes marching on,
your want like an armed warrior.

24.30f.

The vigorous worker, however, must beware of self-sufficiency. When he is advised to 'roll his works to the Lord', one wonders if the picture is of a scribe who rolls out a scroll of plans before his master, or perhaps of a merchant who rolls out material for the approval of a customer, thus:

Roll out your works before the Lord,
that your thoughts may be approved.

16.3

When Qohelet reflected on the end of human life and activity in death, he did not conclude that work was pointless. It is a gift from God's hand to find enjoyment in work; there is nothing better (Eccles. 2.24; 3.13, 22). It is beautiful (5.18–20). Let it be done with zest while its due time lasts, before the end of activity in death (which Qohelet pictures in the old tradition as the universal place of silence, darkness and stillness):

All that your hand finds (prepared for it) to do,
do it with your strength,
for there is no work or plan or knowledge or wisdom
in the Underworld where you are going.

Eccles. 9.10

Ben Sira has much to say about various kinds of work. There was an old tradition, going back to ancient Egypt, of comparing the manual workers unfavourably with the skilled administrative class. Egyptian students often copied a text which depicted the metal worker, for example, as having fingers hard and horny like crocodiles and as stinking worse than fish-roe. The trader sailing down to the Delta is bitten to death by mosquitos. Stone-mason, barber, builder, gardener, farmer, weaver, arrow-maker, courier, embalmer, cobbler, laundryman, bird-catcher, fisherman – all labour long for little reward.[111] Ben Sira is influenced by this tradition, but does not use its tone of ridicule for manual workers. He expects his disciples to be ready for a share of physical work:

> Do not resent manual labour or farm work,
> for these were created by the Most High.
>
> Ecclus. 7.15

It is the same with physicians, who were sometimes in general disrepute: even the best were bound for hell according to the Mishna (Kiddushim 4.14). But Ben Sira would have them honoured, as created for their service by God (38.1f.). Through them the Lord's healing goes out across the face of the earth. The craftsmen, too, should be respected (38.24f.). Their work is long and arduous, absorbing all their attention and strength: workers in precious stones and metals, smiths, potters. They are not suited to high councils or the judiciary; they cannot deploy proverbs like the trained sage. But without them a city could not be inhabited. They maintain the fabric of the world and their prayer is in their work.

Ben Sira presents the work of the learned scribe as turning upon prayer. He must study scripture and search the wisdom of the ancients. Skilled in proverbs, he does practical service also for rulers, even errands to foreign peoples. For all this he seeks the spirit of wisdom in prayer. Through the granting of his prayer he will be able to counsel, meditate, teach, and utter God's praise (39.1–11). All this needs a dedication which must take him from other pursuits:

> The wisdom of the scribe depends on the opportunity
> of leisure.
> Anyone who is to become wise must have little
> other business.
>
> 38.24

But such dedication was not understood to mean complete severance from manual work. Just as the learned student St Paul laboured at making tents (Acts 18.3), so the Sayings of the Fathers recommends that study be combined with the 'way of the earth', ordinary toil. Without it, scripture study would end in failure and sin (2.2). All work is for the divine Master:

> Know before whom you labour,
> and who is the master of your work
> to give you the wages of your toil.
>
> 2.19

> The day is short and the work is great . . .
> and the master of the house is urgent.
>
> 2.20

The Israelite sages, aware of the vanity of human ambition and effort, highly valued work done in humble awareness of God's work. Such human work deserved vigour and enthusiasm. It was a means of joy, health and life.

Trust

Recognizing the limits of their own understanding and abilities, contemplatives are freed to put their trust in God. For their goal of communion with him, the trust which is fundamental in all personal relations must be pervasive in their lives. It is a childlike trust, which sustains them in times of great peril or deprivation. When looking to the future, it may be called hope.

Expounding the encounter with God in contemplation, St Thomas Aquinas (c. 1225–1274) speaks of the darkness when earthly ties are left and all that moves on the human side is the will's desire for God, a bare readiness to wait in hope and longing.[112] Meister Eckhart (c. 1260–1327) saw the contemplative goal as the finding of God in all life and activity, so that the lover of God would be everywhere at home. A trusting, open attitude to God must displace the self's longing for dominion and possession. So the self enters into God's life and works his works.[113]

The theme of trust is strong in Proverbs. It is a matter of being alive to God: sensitive, open, aware towards him, and so delivered from the illusions of self-reliance and vanity:

> Trust in the Lord with all your heart
> and do not lean on your own wisdom.
> Know him in all your ways
> and he will clear your paths.

> Do not be wise in your own eyes,
> fear the Lord and shun evil.
>
> Prov. 3.5f.

Such trust could be developed in meditation. The stilling of the restless self opened the way to awareness of God and to trust and hope in him:

> Whoever ponders a matter will find good,
> and trusting in the Lord, how happy he shall be!
>
> 16.20

There was a sense of salvation in this trust, releasing from that hunted feeling which fear creates:

> Fear of man lays a snare,
> but whoever trusts in the Lord shall be secure.
>
> 29.25

The name of the Lord, by which the needy call to him, is like a high fortress; the righteous run into it and are secure (18.10). The sage's awareness of God, his 'fear of the Lord', is likewise a place of glorious confidence, a homely shelter (14.26). Like metal from the refiner's fire, the promises of God are pure and trustworthy, and he is a shield to those who shelter in him (30.5).

The trust can appear as 'waiting' for the Lord, steadfastly 'hoping' in him. You should not repay an injury, but 'wait for the Lord and he will save you' (20.22). The hope of the righteous ends in joy (10.28). Wisdom, hope and fulfilment belong together (24.13–14). Beginning on the path of wisdom is like seeing the first glimmer of dawn; the darkness begins to yield and hope gradually comes to fulfilment:

> The path of the righteous is like the gleam of dawn
> which grows ever brighter till day is fully come.
>
> 4.18

Von Rad connects this teaching of trust in the Lord with the whole stance of the sages towards the world. God's truth in the world could not become the mere object of man's theoretical knowledge. Reliable knowledge could only be received through a relation of trust with things, letting them retain their puzzling nature, allowing them to speak to us and set us to rights.[114]

In its own way the drama of Job turns on this issue. Job's friends have not the trust to let the truth retain its puzzling nature. They have their explanation ready to master the situation – Job must have grossly sinned in secret. Job, however, trusts at a profound level. Underlying all his bitter lamentation is his trust in truth, in God. Now and then the pounding waves part to reveal this rock:

> He breaks me with breach upon breach,
> running to attack me like a warrior . . .
> Earth, do not cover my blood
> and never let my cry be buried!
> Even now my witness is in heaven,
> he who will testify for me is on high.
> While my earthly friends abuse me,
> to God my eye is weeping . . .
> Oh, lay down a pledge for me with yourself!
> Who else will give bail for me?
>
> Job 16.14–17.3

In all the contradictions he endures he still trusts that truth and goodness will have the last word:

> My closest friends abhor me,
> and those I loved have turned against me . . .
> You my friends, have pity, have pity on me,
> for the hand of God has struck me.
> Must you persecute me like God?
> When will you have enough of slandering me?

> Oh that my defence could be so written,
> cut deep in an inscription
> with iron tool and filling of lead,
> hewn in the rock for ever!
> Yet I know that my champion lives,
> and afterwards he will stand up on the dust,
> and though my skin be consumed,
> my flesh gone, yet I shall see God,
> and I shall see him on my side,
> and my eyes shall see him, estranged from me no more –
> my heart faints within me for longing.
>
> 19.19f.

The knowledge of God

The fulfilment of contemplation is knowledge of God, in the sense of a direct meeting and communion. Plato expressed it as contemplation (*theoria*) of the Beautiful or Good, which is the highest of the eternal real forms beyond the fleeting shadows of sensual experience. Following the path of purification, re-attuning to the eternal world, the soul might suddenly be granted this participatory vision of ultimate unity and meaning, a joyous ecstasy, a home-coming, a reunion.[115] Plotinus developed Plato's teaching. The One who is the fulfilment of contemplation was now shown more clearly as source of all, to which all strove to return. In a movement of longing, all things were returning towards this final contemplation, each attaining in its own way and degree.[116]

The Jewish Philo brought a contribution affected by the Old Testament: the One preserved an inaccessibility in himself, but let himself be known in forms and acts of revelation. Such revelation was granted especially to those who contemplated the universe with the inward eye and yearned constantly for wisdom.[117]

The early Christian teachers of the spiritual path were able to speak more positively about 'knowing God' because of their belief in his reaching out through Christ. The great scholar Origen drew on St John's Gospel for his teaching of 'the Word' (*logos*) – the wisdom, thought and expression of God which became 'flesh' in Jesus. As the believer was taken into the life of Christ, so he was led towards that intimate relation which the eternal Word had with the Father. United with the Word through contemplation, the disciple shared in the Word's own contemplation of God. Through the grace of the Word, he knew God, was known of him, and was made like him.[118]

Gregory of Nyssa (c. 330–395) resumed something of Philo's tendency, stressing the distinction between Creator and creatures and the darkness that surrounded the unknowable God. By God's grace, however, there was still a drawing together. Through ever deeper darkness the soul found the immediate presence of God and knew him, the Unknowable, but only as love knows.[119] We have already traced themes of spiritual darkness in Denys and St John of the Cross; it was this latter who defined contemplation as 'knowledge through love'.[120]

The teaching of union with Christ remained central for contemplative Christians. In fourteenth-century England, for example, we have Walter Hilton: 'Every reasonable soul ought with all its might to covet nighing to Jesus and oneing with him, through feeling his gracious and invisible presence.'[121] And Lady Julian: 'Till I am substantially oned to him, I may never have full rest or true bliss.'[122] Thomas Merton, summarizing centuries of Christian life, draws the connection firmly from contemplation to knowledge of God. Through meditation we learn to withdraw from the confusions of temporal life and so become aware of the presence of God. The outcome is a state of almost constant loving attention to God and dependence on him. Contemplation is the reason for our creation, writes Merton. By it we know and love God as he is in himself.[123] It is that wisdom which makes us friends of God.[124]

Such indescribable contact with the One is often associated with a vision of the unity of all. It is as though the divine order in all things, hidden from the outward eye, were suddenly made manifest – in the words of Thomas Traherne (1637–1674):

> The world resembled his eternity
> in which my soul did walk,
> and everything that I did see
> did with me talk.[125]

It is this realization of hidden unity and the participation in it which is characteristic of eastern contemplatives. 'Hold fast to the unity', taught Lao Tzu in China, meaning the Tao that underlies and imperceptibly governs all existence:

> Tao is all-pervading . . . fathomless,
> like the fountain-head of all things.[126]

> The Great Tao flows everywhere . . .
> the myriad things derive their life from it.[127]

The value of *wu-wei*, 'non-action', was bound up with this intuition of the oneness. Alive to this divine order, the noble person acts only in humility with it.[128]

In Indian religion, as often in the Upanishads, the goal is union with the universal ground and spirit, Brahman. Yoga, the discipline of meditation, is the 'yoke' which makes for this union. The Buddha's Eightfold Path culminated in the 'right meditation' which brings universal consciousness, insight into the hidden nature of all things, participation in the all.[129] Drawing together Hindu and Buddhist threads, the Gita includes a description of an overwhelming vision of God. Its last poem describes how, by a path of unselfishness and love, we come to wisdom, vision of universal order, and union with God:

> When one sees eternity in things that pass away
> and infinity in finite things,
> then one has pure knowledge.

> When a man dwells in the solitude of silence
> and meditation and contemplation are ever with him . . .
> when his selfishness and violence and pride are gone,
> when lust and anger and greediness are no more
> and he is free from the thought 'this is mine',
> then this man has ascended the mountain of the Highest,
> he is worthy to be one with Brahman, with God.
> He is one with Brahman, with God,
> and beyond grief and desire his soul is in peace.
> His love is one for all creation
> and he has supreme love for me.

> By love he knows me in truth,
> who I am and what I am.
> And when he knows me in truth
> he enters into my being.
> In whatever work he does he can shelter in me,
> and by my grace he attains the imperishable home
>   of eternity.[130]

The unitive vision is attested also by Kabir:

> O Kabir
> In a dream,
> God and His creation
> Seem all
> So fragmented.

> But ah, in the light
> Of the day,
> One sees the unity
> Of all things![131]

Fed by long currents of east and west, modern poets too have written movingly of realization of the universal divine order and the awesome, all-satisfying Presence. From his contemplation of the great sea, Walt Whitman is led to voyage into the infinite seas of God:

> O vast Rondure, swimming in space,
> covered all over with visible power and beauty,
> alternate light and day and the teeming spiritual darkness,
> unspeakable high processions of sun and moon and
> countless stars above . . .
> Bathe me, O God, in thee, mounting to thee,
> I and my soul to range in range of thee.
>
> O thou transcendent,
> nameless, the fibre and the breath,
> light of the light, shedding forth universes, thou centre
> of them,
> swiftly I shrivel at the thought of God . . .[132]

These little examples of our theme, culled from east and west, from times distant and near, are but a hinting at what cannot be described. Beyond concepts, beyond images, words must be few and inadequate. Those who classify religious experience can go very wrong if they treat expressions of the fulfilment of contemplation like legal statements and make absolute distinctions. From such a misjudged approach perhaps comes the opinion of Dean Inge in his Bampton Lectures of 1899. Taking mysticism as the attempt to realize the presence of the living God in the soul and in nature, he judged that the Jewish mind and character were alien to it. He could find traces of such mysticism in Jeremiah, Isaiah and Psalms, but he found nothing in the wisdom books.[133] Indeed he thought Job illustrated the very opposite:

> Here is no joining of God and man, but only absolute submission to a law which is entirely outside us and beyond our comprehension. Such is the final lesson of Job, illustrat-

ing that view of the relation of man to God with which man can never be content.[134]

There is surely a misreading here. The culmination of Job's quest is not 'absolute submission to a law' but the contemplative experience as expressed by Walter Hilton: nothing other than a sight of the Lord, which is true peace.[135]

Through his long dark night of honesty, Job has steadfastly rejected illusions and in naked truth sought God. At last God has appeared and spoken to him from a storm. He has not spoken directly of Job's case, but of wonders great and small in Nature, observed as by the contemplative eye in beauty, love and wonder, and conjured up as by a poet. Appropriately, Job's words of response are very few (42.1–6):

> . . . I had heard of you only by hearsay,
> but now my own eyes have seen you . . .

This seeing of God fulfils his earlier intuition:

> I shall see God,
> and I shall see him on my side,
> and my eyes shall see him, estranged from me no more –
> my heart faints within me for longing.
>
> 19.26f.

Thomas Merton describes contemplation as 'at once the existential appreciation of our own "nothingness" and of the divine reality, perceived by ineffable spiritual contact within the depths of our own being'.[136] In Job's case, too, there comes with his beholding of God a sense of utter 'nothingness', unworthiness. He has no inclination now to argue his case; only to express briefly his self-abasement and his wonder at his direct sight of God, and then to abide in silence. In 42.6 the Hebrew verbs would normally mean 'I reject and repent'. The first verb, however, can be better explained here as 'melt', and the second as linked on to express the sense of a new outlook, tinged with the sorrow of creaturely unworthiness, yet passing into the deep peace of reconciliation:[137]

I had heard of you only by hearsay,
but now my own eyes have seen you.
Therefore I melt away sorrowing
on the dust and ashes.

42.5–6

It is indeed remarkable that this great wisdom book, which has given expression to the deepest agony and hope in the human condition in the form of a drama, should have made the plot turn on such seeing of God. No explanation of Job's suffering, no spiritual counsel or comfort does God give. What the audience knows of heaven's purpose is never told to Job. No theory of the world's evils is established. The terrible crisis is built up, every resource of religion and philosophy is used in vain to alleviate it, and the resolution comes at last in God's showing himself to Job. It is direct, ineffable contact, and Job enters a new life.

But what a difficult task for a dramatist! How to stage the ultimate mystery of the soul that is granted sight of God? The author found his answer in seas and deserts, the beauty of morning, the unspeakable high processions of light and dark and the hosts of heaven, snow and hail and rain, thunder and lightning, dew and frost, and the wise life of animals and birds in their generations, and the primaeval mysterious ones (40.15f.) that are never seen but sensed, dread powers held safe by God. By these, in contemplation and poetry, he signified the power of the disclosure of God to Job. Can we not say, then, that Job's sight of God was accompanied by an intuition of cosmic order, a unity of wondrous life manifesting the divine wisdom?

If we look further in the Israelite wisdom books for experience of contact with the divine, we can take first the uncanny visitation in the night which Job's friend Eliphaz recounts (4.12f.). The world lay deep in slumber. Uneasily stirring, troubled by the imagery of his dreams, Eliphaz suddenly heard the slightest rustle, which he felt to be a presence from above:

Fear and trembling seized me,
sending terror through all my bones.
The hair of my flesh stood up
as a Spirit glided before my face.
He stood still, but I could not discern his face,
a shape was before my eyes.

As Elijah had heard a mere whisper of a voice (*qol demama daqqa*) when the Lord came to him on the holy mountain (I Kings 19.12), so the old sage too heard a whisper of a voice (*demama wa-qol*). It spoke to him of the awful purity of God which shamed even angels.

The passage illustrates how vision was thought to inform the counsels of the sages. There is indeed a proverb which says outright:

> Where there is no vision, a people breaks loose,
> but happy the one that heeds direction.
>
> Prov. 29.18

Another proverb tells of the lamp of God which shines deep in the cavities of the body, examining, filling the soul with interior light:

> The lamp of the Lord, (as) the breath of man,
> searches all the chambers of the belly.
>
> 20.27

In these examples we gain the impression of wisdom teachers who knew the power of God within and about them, and who were ready if he chose to grant them knowledge of himself.

In our section on the theme of 'love', we considered passages in Proverbs, Job, Ecclesiasticus and the Wisdom of Solomon that portray Wisdom as a person. She has two main roles: firstly in divine creation, and secondly as teacher, guide and helper of mankind.

In Job 28 we have a self-contained poem about the inaccessibility of this Wisdom. The grasping, questing human race, with all its marvels of technology, cannot track her down, seize her and possess her. Her secret is open only to God:

> For he looks to the ends of the earth,
> he sees under the whole heavens.
> When he determined the weight of the wind
> and meted out the waters with a measure,
> when he made decree for the rain
> and the way of lightning and thunder,
> then he beheld her and knew her fully,
> he contemplated[138] and studied her deeply.
>
> 28.24f.

This Wisdom, then, is the Creator's thought, plan and skill which give form and order in the universe. It seems that the human experience of invention – the recognition of a thought that seems to be outside of oneself – has provided a helpful model. The Creator has thus struck upon an idea, envisaged his plan, checked and reviewed it, and embodied it in the marvels of creation. It is in the world, but is uniquely of him; found in created things, yet no ordinary creature; a divine secret and presence, everywhere; yet, for grasping men, nowhere to be found.

The personality of this presence is felt strongly in the great passage of Proverbs 8. Here Wisdom raises her voice and calls to the crowds as they battle at their getting and spending. Again the association with creation is emphasized. Before the great elements could be given substance and form, the Creator had to engender his plan, give birth to his idea, which then assisted him joyously in all his work, delighting his heart:

> The Lord begot me in the beginning of his way,
> preceding his works, at the outset.
> In the dawn of time I was woven for birth,
> in the beginning, before earth existed.
> When there were no oceans I was brought to birth,
> when there were no springs heavy with water.
> Before the mountain bases were sunk,
> before the hills I was born,
> when as yet he had not made earth and its spaces
> and the high edges of the land.
> When he set up the heavens I was there,
> when he drew a circle on the face of the deep,
> when he fixed the skies above,
> when he established the springs of the ocean,
> when he appointed the sea its law
> and the waters, not to pass the limit he had spoken,
> when he marked out the foundations of the earth –
> then I was at his side, his skilled assistant,
> and I was his delight day by day,
> dancing before him all the time,
> playing through the good land of his earth,
> delighting in the children of Adam.
>
> Prov. 8.22f.

What a wonderful voice to hear amidst a city throng! It is as
though the poet had come into the busy gateway from the
deep silence of the wilderness; as though the sweet voice he
had heard from beyond, as he contemplated the sunrise or a
shy animal, still sounded in his heart, sounded all the clearer
amid the clatter because the message was so needed. Like the
poet of Job, he had mystical knowledge of divine meaning in
the world, the first-born Thought which was prior to all
things, attended their creation, suffused the world with
playful joy, and took loving delight in our race. His account
dwells long on the Beginning, as though Wisdom opened to
the devoted sage the primal simplicity, the air of dawn, the
merry heart of the child. But the primeval simplicity is also the
warrant of authority. This Wisdom is prior to all that God has
made; she has precedence; her call deserves all heed.

The jostling throng in the spaces by the gateway sets all its
concern on lesser things. But if any will pause and listen to
Wisdom's call, she will teach him the true way of life:

> Happy the one who listens to me,
> watching every day at my doors,
> on guard at my entrance-posts . . .
> for to find me is to find life
> and gain acceptance with the Lord.
>
> 8.33f.

As we read over the various passages where Wisdom
appears as a person, we can appreciate the mystical dimension which belonged essentially to the way taught by the
sages. The good disciple took this way of ethics, discipline and
meditation and entered a relationship with Wisdom. Such
warmth and devotion were there that it could appropriately be
described as a personal relationship, indeed the way of a
lover. It was a revelation of world-meaning and an entrance
into knowledge of God. Much as we love our modern
education, we could hardly speak of it so. But for the ancient
sages, the way of Wisdom led into divine mystery. One who
contemplated Wisdom and pondered her secrets would dwell
in the midst of glory (Ecclus. 14.20–27).

There remains another indication, widespread in their sayings, that the sages saw life as contemplatives who have known

contact with God. This is the large number of references to 'the fear of the Lord'. A profound experience, such as bereavement or falling in love, will often cause us to see everything with changed eyes. The world, as it were, has a different colour. In the same way, contemplatives who have known some moment of divine immediacy turn again to all life with new eyes, because they remain in constant awareness of God. Such awareness can be traced in the sages' use of the phrase 'the fear of the Lord'. The Desert Fathers have a use of this kind. 'Always have the fear of God before your eyes', taught Abba Anthony,[139] and Abba James related this fear to an inner illumination which affects all one's character and conduct:

> Just as a lamp lights up a dark room, the fear of God, when it penetrates a person's heart, illuminates him, teaching him all the virtues and commandments of God.[140]

A saying of one of Job's friends illustrates how the fear of God and contemplation could be coupled together. Job's bitter words, complains Eliphaz, would damage the fear of God and hinder meditation before him (Job 15.4). In Proverbs 'the fear of the Lord' is the 'beginning of wisdom' (9.10) and the 'beginning (or chief part) of knowledge' (1.7). It is the 'discipline (or instruction) of wisdom' (15.33). It is 'to know him in all your ways' (3.6–7), and is 'healing to your navel and medicine to your bones' (3.8). Significantly, it is also described as the goal of the disciple's long course of attention, prayer and eager search, and is coupled with 'knowledge of God':

> My son, if you receive my sayings
> and store up my instructions,
> making your ear attentive to Wisdom
> and inclining your heart to understanding,
> yes, if you cry out for insight
> and raise your voice to beg understanding,
> if you seek her like silver
> and search for her as for hidden treasure,
> then you will discern the fear of the Lord
> and find the knowledge of God.
>
> 2.1–5

For Qohelet the fear of the Lord arises not from consideration of the terrible power of God, but from contemplation of
the perfection of his work. Beyond the haze of 'vanity' –
fleeting values and seeming absurdities – the sage gains
knowledge of eternity, perfection, in the work of God; so he
finds a life of given joy in awareness, 'fear', of him:

> I know that everything that God does
> is for ever,
> there is nothing to add,
> and nothing to take from it,
> and God has done it
> so that they shall fear before him.
>
> Eccles. 3.14

And Qohelet also teaches that, from all life's contradictions,
only the fear of God can bring us out (7.18).

Sayings in Job (28.28) and Ecclesiasticus (1.27; 19.20) state
simply that 'the fear of the Lord is wisdom'. Waxing more
eloquent, Ben Sira also says it is 'the beginning of wisdom',
'the full measure of wisdom', 'the crown of wisdom', and 'the
root of wisdom' (1.11f.). He also says that 'the fear of the Lord
surpasses everything' (25.11).

'The fear of the Lord', then, is a pervading value in Israelite
wisdom. Von Rad goes so far as to say that all the proverbs
presuppose it.[141] It meant a constant awareness of the reality
of God, an awe that affected every moment and impulse in the
life of the wise. Surely the vitality and prominence of this
element of teaching arose from 'knowledge of God', contact
with the divine. It would otherwise be only a superficial
moralizing idea which could not have taken its present place
in the literature.

Not to every sage or disciple would God make himself
known as dramatically as he did to Job. But the way of
wisdom, it seems, brought moments of contact sufficient to
illumine the rest, so that the whole way was a progress into
'the fear of the Lord' and 'knowledge of God'. We may
compare what Evelyn Underhill says of the mystic's way as
'the art of union with Reality'. This union, she writes,

> represents not so much a rare and unimaginable operation,
> as something which he is doing, in a vague, imperfect

fashion, at every moment of his conscious life, and is doing with intensity and thoroughness in all the more valid moments of that life.[142]

Connecting our themes

The main themes of the Old Testament wisdom books have now been considered. Each was introduced with relevant samples from the world's contemplative literature. The bringing together of such texts has helped to clarify particular themes. It has also helped to show a pattern of spiritual life, a dedicated life of response to eternal reality.

For the themes we have traced are by no means unrelated. They are woven into one texture – a pattern of life lived with quiet and receptive awe before God, the Lord of the mysterious and marvellous universal order.

Under a master-sage or spiritual father the disciple learnt the value of discipline and reproof, and that modesty of requirements which makes space for meditation. He was nourished on poetry: beautiful and truthful sayings that were sweetness to the soul and medicine to the bones. He acquired the 'listening heart'; he came to be 'on watch', attentive to God and to the wonders of all life, not deafened by the clamour of a dominating self. So he found the way of humility, openness to the Lord, and love. From this disposition arose restraint in speaking of God. The truly listening, humble, loving heart alone could know 'how small a whisper do we hear of him'. Here it seemed well that words be few and meditative silence much.

The wise heart was ready to recognize at every turn the gifts and appointments of God. Work was his gift, and so was the spouse's love, and gracious Wisdom, and life itself.

But there was no poetry, no attention, no rich silence without honesty. Better to feel the ferocity of God and the futility of the world than 'be fed what is not him'. Thus the travellers on Wisdom's path reach the dark night of the soul. Their only stay is trust – trust in the Lord or, if he is gone from all knowledge, trust in the truth. At last the night gives way to dawn; the light grows more and more till the day is full come. In one way or another God makes himself known, and the awe of him, the sense of his immediacy, remains to colour every moment. The whole quest for wisdom becomes a journey into immediacy with God. Wisdom herself, God's Thought underlying all that exists, takes the pilgrim into a loving divine friendship, gives him the breath of early dawn and a healing vision of cosmic order.

Jacques Maritain has said of creativity in art that it involves an asceticism and a purifying suffering of its own. The artists, 'whose style of life is active, will have the grace of contemplation, but of a masked, unapparent contemplation'.[143] The Israelite sages remain close to the bustle of the world. Many of their sayings have an earthy quality. They are concerned with conduct in family relations, in the market, in society. Their contemplation may well seem 'masked, unapparent', and indeed has often escaped the notice of modern readers.

But the distinction between the 'active' and 'contemplative' life was not always as sharp as presented in some Christian tradition. We have noted how the Chinese Taoists followed a mystical path while affirming nature and the world; they saw the sage as the ideal ruler. Confucius likewise believed that the supreme sages had founded dynasties, while those near to them in wisdom became prime ministers. We saw how the Hindu sage expected his pupils to apportion their life in stages, worldly and unworldly. Like the Chinese, Plato thought of the contemplative as the ideal ruler: no one without the contemplative vision, he thought, could act with wisdom either in his own life or in matters of state.[144]

The Israelite sages, then, are not extraordinary in being contemplatives who are not cut off from 'action'. Their beloved Wisdom is the very power of good government (Prov. 8.15–16). Work is their satisfaction and joy. This Wisdom for which they watch and pray, study and meditate, they aptly describe as 'the fountain of life' (16.11; cf. 3.18; 10.11; 13.14; 14.27).

3

WISDOM AND CONTEMPLATION IN THE PSALMS

We noted at the outset that wisdom writings in the Old Testament had a distinctive character connected with a tradition of schooling. Akin to the philosophies of Egypt and Mesopotamia, they tended to view human life in universal, non-national terms. But if they were thus distinctive in the Old Testament, they were not tightly shut off from the other religious currents of Israel. Indeed, the kings, princes, priests and prophets who took the lead in the public religion would be likely to have studied in the wisdom schools.

It is not surprising, therefore, that the influence of the sages can be observed in many parts of the Old Testament. Especially in the Book of Psalms there is evidence of a contemplative wisdom like that which we have found in the wisdom books. This we shall explore in the present chapter.

Contacts between the Psalms and wisdom teaching are generally acknowledged. Some psalms indeed are commonly classified by scholars as 'wisdom poems', such as Psalms 1, 37, 112, 127. Such psalms distinctively have the form of teaching, rather than of praise or prayer. They make summary observations in the manner of proverbs and, like the proverbs, often refer to the contrasting destinies of the good and the wicked, the need for quiet trust and the fear of the Lord. Even outside the acknowledged 'wisdom poems', there are quite a few psalms where we feel close to the wisdom teachers, as for example in the great Psalm 104:

> How manifold your creatures, Lord!
> Through Wisdom you have made them all.
>
> Psalm 104.24

Surprisingly then, we find that what appeared to be two contrasting circles – sages who hardly refer to religious institutions and psalmists who serve in temple worship – share important territory of the spirit.

Turning now to the psalms in question, we shall explore what these much loved and much-used poems reveal of the life of contemplation, the disciplined way of attention, the direct, ineffable contact with God.

The contemplative musician

A meditative singer has been beautifully portrayed for us on a stone relief that has been recovered from an ancient tomb in Saqqara, Egypt. He is a blind man with close-shaven head and a tunic gathered in pleats round loins and upper arms. He sits back on his heels with the large harp resting on his knees. With both hands he plays the strings to accompany his song. He holds his head erect and the lines of his face suggest how he sings with a soft nasal tone. His whole posture and expression are those of deep concentration and adoration.[1]

In a similar spirit, the Hebrew musicians with lyre or harp offered up meditative psalms. Music was considered to be like prophecy, an inspiration from God (I Chron. 25). Given from heaven, it was fitted to be offered back, easily passing into the beyond, pleasing to the Lord (Ps. 104.33–34). Expressing the praise of God, it focussed the mind on him and fostered communion and rapture. It was filled with his name and his presence (118.14). Comparison can be made with mediaeval Sufis who gathered in *sama‘* houses to hear the singing of litanies based on the Quran or the names of God, achieving a concentration that opened the way to the interior silence of communion.[2]

The favourite instrument of the psalmists, the lyre (137.2), was sweet (81.2) and healing (I Sam. 16.23). Its notes led the heart into a deep tranquillity and inner light, unlocking the riddles of existence which had threatened to frustrate the good way (Ps. 49.4). Passing lightly to and from the beyond, it seemed a language of all the elements of the universe. In music all creatures joined together in looking to God (98; 148; 150). Here was enjoyment of the great unity, the ultimate harmony.[3]

The course of the meditation of one such musician is beautifully preserved in Psalm 19. When he tells of 'the resounding' of his heart rising with the song of his mouth (19.14), we sense that he is at one with his resounding instrument which lies against his body. He seems to be kneeling in the open court of the temple, where most worship took place, and so open to the heavens and rising sun on which he meditates at the beginning of his psalm. Other psalmists tell of gazing at the night sky (8.3) and of arousing harp and lyre in sympathy with the rising dawn (57.8–10). For Psalm 19, then, it is reasonable to trace a meditation which began when the firmament was filled with the starry hosts (19.1) and continued till the jubilant sun came forth (19.5–6) and the priests offered the morning sacrifice in the same court in prayer for God's 'favour' (cf. 19.14).

The night sky is a silent splendour. The crowded brilliance is all the more striking in the usually clear atmosphere of Jerusalem. But all is in silence. Our psalmist will have passed through a long silence of meditation to reach his knowledge of the music beyond the silence. Beyond ordinary hearing, he heard the stars singing, pouring out to each other a testimony praising the Creator:

> The heavens are telling the glory of God
> and the sky declares the deeds of his hands.
> Each day pours out song to the next
> and one night to another unfolds knowledge.
> No human phrase or word do they use,
> their voice is not for earthly ears,
> but their music goes out through all the earth
> and their words to the ends of the world.
>
> 19.1–4

The night passed and the sun rose on the psalmist. Over the Mount of Olives came up the strong Jerusalem sun and brought a sense of joy. This Sun – if he had slept through the night, he now came out from his tent with no ordinary waking; he was like the eastern bridegroom coming out from his wedding bower, jubilant and resplendent. Yes, there was joy in this rising, and as he ran his track across the heavens, he would give warmth to every creature.

To some peoples the joyful disk seemed like the face of God. To the Egyptians it was a revelation of the Creator, to the Babylonians the glory of the divine Justice. For our singer it was a model of joyful service to the Lord, and he was struck by its pure brilliance and its giving of light and warmth to all creatures. It brought to mind another sun, a sun of the soul, the Lord's 'law'. And so he began to sing appreciatively of the direction and teaching which the Lord had given, the commands and precepts which led the obedient along the path of good life. And he sang of all this under the impulse which the sun had given his meditation:

> The Lord's law is a perfect whole,
>> restoring soul-strength.
> The Lord's promise is sure,
>> making the simple wise.
> The Lord's precepts are right,
>> making the heart happy.
> The Lord's command is bright,
>> giving light to the eyes.
> Fear of the Lord is clear-shining,
>> ever constant.
> The Lord's rules are truth,
>> altogether just,
> more desirable than gold,
>> than much fine gold,
> sweeter by far than honey
>> fresh from honey-combs.
>
>   19.7f.

In the Lord's guiding law he found a mighty sun. Here was rounded perfection and power to revive a dissipated soul. Here was reliability; here was enlightenment for the simplest, bestowing wisdom. Here were morning rays that delighted the heart. Here was light to guide the eyes. One who was ever alive to this guiding God, having 'fear of the Lord', saw all life illumined and could be constant in all circumstances. Here were golden rays of truth that glittered beyond the finest gold and gave sweetness beyond honey.

The contemplation moves through God's manifestations towards God himself. The singer now addresses his Lord directly and acknowledges the benefit he has himself received from this bright sun of teaching. At once he is aware of his frailty and unworthiness. He asks God to keep him from the sin that creeps in unnoticed, as well as from reckless acts of defiance.

In the great open court the priests would now be offering up the morning sacrifice, with the supplication that they and all the people would be accepted favourably by God. So our singer concludes with the prayer that his music also may ascend as an offering finding God's favour. The psalmists believed that God preferred such a song above all the other temple offerings (69.30–31). May he then be pleased with this chain of meditation that has ascended with instrument and voice, and may he preserve his servant in the bond of contemplation, the knowledge of his saviour:

> May the words of my mouth
> and the resounding of my heart
> come before you for favour,
> Lord, my rock and my redeemer!
>
> 19.14

The contemplative circle

The solitary figure rapt in contemplation is not all that the meditative psalms reveal. Just as tradition told of a whole college of elders sharing with Moses a vision of God (Exod. 24.9–11), so there are indications in the psalms that a group of worshippers could together 'see his glory'.

Psalm 8 is one of those amazing psalms which express so much so briefly. From first to last it is addressed to God, having none of the exhortations to the assembly or the world typical of most psalms of praise. At the beginning and end we hear identical words:

> Yahweh, our Lord,
> how glorious your name in all the world!

This name of God 'Yahweh' (usually rendered throughout the English Old Testament as 'Lord') may mean 'He Is', indicating the absolute sovereign One. In the name, it was felt, God gave himself. By it worshippers could call to him in need or in praise. The proclamation of this name in worship especially betokened his nearness, the new shining of the glory of his presence. The beginning and end of our psalm, then, expresses awareness that the Lord is manifest; his glory is seen to light up the universe.

This visionary awareness is shared by the group, which might be the family of singers, or extend to the great festal assembly. The larger grouping is not improbable, as the festal worship centred round the proclamation of God's revelation in universal sovereignty. All the pilgrims were considered as devotees, prepared in discipline to behold the revelation of God. At all events, the 'our' and the exact repetition of the lines indicate a chorus of voices and their full participation in the thoughts of the inner section of the psalm.

In the inner section we see something of the role of the solitary figure. A single voice tells of a journey of contemplation – 'when I looked at your heavens . . .'. He had been alone, but the thoughts that were given him embraced the whole race, and indeed all creatures. And now, as a member of the fellowship of musicians and worshippers, he was able to draw them all into his meditation and response to God.

In his song he tells how his meditation developed:

> When I looked at your heavens,
> the work of your fingers,
> the moon and the stars
> which you created . . .

8.3

In the wisdom books we often found reference to wonders of nature which move the heart to wisdom and awe of God. The sages considered the wonders till Wisdom herself, the very thought and creative skill of God, called out to them and led them on the way to God. The psalmist likewise has been led by the marvels of the brilliant night sky to deeper relation with God. All in his converse with God, he reflects on 'your heavens', 'your fingers', 'that which you created'. And the overwhelming thought is of how this unspeakably great God should have given honour and care to puny man. By his gift he has made him like a king, ruling the other species, lacking but a little of heavenly glory:

> You have given him little less than heavenly beings,
> and with glory and splendour you have crowned him.
> You have put everything under his feet –
> all sheep and oxen,
> wild animals also,
> birds of the skies and fish of the sea
> and things that crawl the tracks of the seas.
>
> 8.5f.

A special beauty of the Psalms is the uniting of a mystical view of nature with the places, times and customs of worship. In the heart of worship at the temple, the psalmists hear praise that includes the roar of the sea, the singing and dancing of fields and trees (96.11–12). Psalm 8 gives another example. The singer unfolds a mysterious interpretation of worship in the temple:

> You whose glory is chanted above the heavens,
> by the mouth of babes at the breast
> you have founded a fortress against your foes
> to still the enemy and avenger.
>
> 8.1b–2

The baby's first cry is a shout for life. The crying of infants is incoherent, but it is a sign of life. For all the skill of the psalmists, Jerusalem's liturgy, compared with its great subject, is but childish babble. And yet it is a sacrament of life, a bastion for the good meaning of the world against the tides of chaos. For God has chosen the temple mountain and touched it with his holy presence; here he has appointed and empowered worship. He has made it like the threshold of his heavenly dwelling, a place to meet him, a stronghold against the chaos which God mastered as Creator.

And if it is in reality small and vulnerable, and if the worship is inadequate, then what condescension of the Creator is here! As he stoops to raise mankind to him and to care for them, so he stoops to make the temple the means of his grace and to fashion from the praises a bulwark against evil powers.

So from the opening chorus, through the solo, to the final chorus, the group and the leader take a contemplative way in few words. They behold a revelation of God. But they meet the Power of all the universe in his stooping grace, his acceptance, care and crowning of the weak and lowly.

An aid to directing the heart

Credit for outspokenness must be given to B. Duhm, whose commentary on the Psalms (1899/1922) contains some scathing remarks about the longest psalm, 119. Never, he thought, had so much ink been expended to so little purpose:

> What sort of aim the author had in view in the composition of these 176 hexameters, I know not. In any case this 'psalm' is the most empty product that ever blackened paper. With it one could more readily make a heretic weary than with all the seven penitential psalms together. Also from a literary point of view it would be difficult to point to a composition to rival this opus in ineptitude and tedium.[4]

The whole point of the psalm, however, is to sustain a meditation where thought and feeling are reined in and the Lord is contemplated without distraction. The inessential is therefore emptied out.

Like beads on a rosary, a set of names for his revelatory word is told over and over again: his 'instruction' (*tora*), 'testimony', 'precepts', 'statutes', 'commandments', 'ordinances', 'word', 'promise', and we can add 'way' and 'path'. While it is likely that all this guidance from the Lord is thought to centre in sacred rolls which are studied and recited, the psalm does not actually mention any writings or particular laws or observances. When the singer tells of his soul faint with longing for God's ordinances (119.20, 40, 131), watching for his promise (119.123), and wanting God with shining face to teach him his statutes (119.33–34, 85), it is clearly not just a matter of reading a text. The given body of sacred story, commandments, exhortations and promises came to life in communion with the Lord and Saviour. The study and recital of it all was just a part of living from the breath of his lips, a help in keeping oneself before his face, open to his will and spirit.

So the names for his life-giving word are told over and over again, skilfully woven to express a few recurring themes of praise and prayer – warm appreciations of his revelations and guidance, statements of need and trust. And as contemplative prayer is sustained over the counting of beads or fingers, so the psalm sustains its gaze to the self-revealing God by a systematic scheme. For each letter of the alphabet in turn there are eight verses, which each begin with that letter. In this scheme there is no doubt a sense of artistic wholeness and perfection, and an aid to memory and fluent recitation. But above all, the scheme exerts a control of mind and heart in steadfast, undistracted meditation.

It is a remarkably extended communion; almost all the 176 verses are phrased as direct address to God (the exceptions are the introductory verses 1–3, and then 115). The path to him is his 'tora', his teaching and guidance, and the psalm's course of thought holds constantly to this, allowing no deviation. As a religious essay it would be monotonous, repetitious. But as a meditation it rings true and indeed became a classic. In some Christian rounds of prayer, where God's 'word' and 'way' are taken to be his self-expression in Christ, it has been recited daily. The Fathers describe it as 'the Teacher of the faithful, a paradise of all fruits, the storehouse of the Holy Ghost, and just in proportion as it seems easier on the surface, so is it deeper in the abyss of its mysteries'.[5]

Our psalmist refers several times to his meditation:

> In your precepts will I meditate
> and contemplate your ways.
>
> 119.15

> Make me understand the way of your precepts
> and I will meditate upon your marvels.
>
> 119.27

And I will lift up my hands towards your commandments
    which I love,
and I will meditate in your statutes.

119.48

How I love your teaching!
All day long it is my meditation.

119.97

The word used for 'meditate' in these passages is *śiḥ*, which
indicates vocal activity. Intoned reading or recital from
memory of sacred books is probably involved. Also there
would be recital of the name of the Lord and offerings of praise
and prayer in the manner of the psalm itself:

I have recited your name in the night
that I may keep your teaching.

119.55

The free offerings of my mouth receive with favour, Lord,
and teach me your commandments.

119.108

Such 'recital' or 'remembrance' (*zeker*) can be compared with
the *dhikr* in Islam, which involved the repetition of words and
phrases from scripture 'in order to internalize them totally, so
that through the intimacy achieved with God's word, the
divine presence itself might be experienced'.[6]

The psalmist's meditation is an activity begun at set times of
day and night and running virtually unstopped through his
whole existence: 'in the night' (v. 55), 'at midnight' (v. 62),
'before the dawn' (v. 147), 'before the watches of the night'
(v. 148), 'seven times a day' (v. 164), 'with the whole heart'
(vv. 10, 145), 'all the day' (v. 97). But it is not a burden. On the
contrary, he calls it a delight, like the happy play of a child
(vv. 14, 16, 24). It is like singing a song (v. 54), the commandments becoming 'melodies' which enliven this 'traveller's inn'
which is this earthly home (v. 54). His passion for the sacred
lore is because of the communion with the Lord which it gives:

My mouth I open wide and I gasp
in longing for your commandments.
Turn to me and be gracious to me
as is your custom for lovers of your name.

119.131–2

When we were considering the weight given to 'the fear of the Lord' in the wisdom books, it seemed right to link it with the sages' experience of God. The way of wisdom brought moments of contact which filled the life of the wise with a pervading awe. Our psalmist, too, tells of a 'fear' which arises from encounter with the dread Holy One and characterizes his whole way:

> My flesh has bristled in dread of you,
> and I have fear of your commandments.
>
> 119.120

There is a resemblance to the experience of Job's friend, who told how the hairs of his flesh stood up when a spirit appeared to him in the night (Job 4.12f.).

And like Qohelet, the psalmist has seen for all earthly perfection a limit, while the work of God is unsearchable, his commandment exceedingly broad (119.96). In his way and his will there is eternal satisfaction. Sufferings and tribulation abound for the psalmist; men have almost made an end of him, but in God he finds a hiding place and a shield (v. 114). The great meditation ends with earnest plea for the Lord to seek and save him and bring him home:

> May my soul live and praise you
> and may your commandments help me.
> I have wandered like a lost sheep.
> Seek your servant,
> for I have not forgotten your ordinances.
>
> 119.175–6

Roots of meditation

An inspiring model of contemplative study can be seen in Confucianism. Rodney Taylor describes how important here is the exercise of study in the slow progress along the sagely path. The scholar may sit quietly copying with his brush some phrase from a Confucian classic. He is serious but rejoices in the perfection of the text and its characters. Incense burns before the picture of his teacher. In his simple, respectful task of copying he lives the religious life.[7]

In similar spirit, the ancient Egyptian scribe learned ardently to love writing.[8] He was told:

> Copy your fathers and your ancestors . . .
> Behold, their words remain in writing.
> Open, that you may read and copy their wisdom.
> Thus the skilled man becomes learned.[9]

The Hebrew practice of meditative study which we have already discerned in Psalm 119 comes into view also in Psalm 1. This little psalm is particularly close to the wisdom books: its form is instruction to pupils rather than an address to God; in proverb style it uses the sharp contrast of righteous and wicked; it centres on imagery of tree and chaff, and it pictures life as a chosen 'way'. It seems to have been placed at the head when the collection of psalms was already well grown. Thus it shows us what was felt to be suitable as preface to the great book.

It focuses on the individual and his pattern of life. With all the warmth at his command, the sage recommends to his disciple a fruitful, valid way, and warns him against a way that ends only in the desert of the lost. By the right way the disciple will come through life's ordeals and have part in the divine community.

What is this good way? It is described with just one feature. Avoiding the way of the hardened scoffers, the sage delights in the Lord's guidance, his *tora*, meditating in it day and night. The verb used here for 'meditating' (*haga*) involves a murmuring sound. The teachings are recited from memory or from a scroll. Constant meditation in this fashion fixed the heart on God and his will, feeding the soul with his spirit and thought. The meditation expresses an attitude of desire for God and sheer delight in him:

> His pleasure is in the Lord's guidance,
> and in his guidance he meditates day and night.
>
> 1.2

The sage now encourages his disciple by putting before him a strong image of the value of such meditation. It is an image of life. In the near eastern climate the culture of trees needed much care, especially to ensure a constant supply of water. A sapling might be transplanted to a garden where channels of water, ideally from a perpetual spring, might nourish its roots. One who constantly meditates on the Lord's teachings is likewise said to be drawing up life-giving grace through the roots of his being. Nourished by continual communion with the Creator, he becomes a fruitful person:

> He shall be like a tree transplanted by channels of water,
> which gives its fruit at its right time
> and its leaves do not wither.
> Yes, in all that he does he prospers.

1.3

To this an opposing picture is added. The end of the scoffer's way is summarized in an image of transience and waste. The harvester tosses his threshed corn into the breeze; the good, heavy grain falls at his feet, but the light straw and husks are whirled away. Thus the wicked:

> They are like the chaff
> which the wind drives away.

1.4

But while the wicked court death by despising the very spring of life, it is not just a matter of natural processes. They offend the Judge of the world, who personally upholds the good values of his teaching:

> Therefore the wicked will not stand in the judgment,
> nor sinners in the assembly of the righteous.

1.5

The psalm sums it all up still more succinctly with the picture of the alternative ways (1.6). God 'knows' the good way, the way of meditation and openness to his will. He is present there with those who take it, caring for them, guiding them to their goal. But the other way leads away from him. Its travellers ignore or despise his instruction and lose themselves in a waste land.

This little poem, prefacing the Book of Psalms, seems thus to have been positioned by heirs of the wisdom schools who regarded the collection as part of the Lord's guidance in the way of wisdom. In reciting psalms the disciple could enjoy constant contact with the Lord, realized in devotion to his will.

The psalms themselves were seen as part of his 'instruction', *tora*, from which one drank with delight and received abundant life.

The sages in question will probably be of the later period, part of the development which leads to Ben Sira. We have seen how he was a true wisdom teacher, but one for whom it was natural to link wisdom with God's *tora*. He is a clear figure in a clearly known period around 200 BC. The flowing together of the currents of wisdom schooling and *tora* piety, however, had probably happened gradually over many centuries. Around the sixth century Moses is represented as saying:

> See, I have taught you statutes and ordinances as the Lord my God commanded me . . . and if you keep them and do them, that will be your wisdom and your understanding in the eyes of the peoples . . .
>
> Deut. 4.5–6

In the spirit of Psalms 1, 19, 119, other leaders were pictured as vocally and continually meditating in the Lord's law, learning 'the fear of the Lord'. Thus Joshua is instructed:

> This book of *tora* shall not depart out of your mouth, and you shall meditate (*haga*) in it day and night, that you may observe to do all that is written in it, for then you shall make your way prosper and then you will succeed.
>
> Josh. 1.8

And in similar way the king is to take the path of humility and holy fear:

> And it shall be, when he sits on the throne of his kingdom, that he shall write himself a copy of this *tora* according to a scroll from the keeping of the levite-priests. And it shall be with him, and he shall read in it all the days of his life, that he may learn to fear the Lord his God in keeping all the words of this *tora* and these statutes to do them. So his heart will not be above his brothers and he will not turn aside from the commandments to right or left . . .
>
> Deut. 17.18–20

What is especially interesting about the union of wisdom and law piety is the ideal, especially strong in the psalms, that the Lord's instruction is not only to be learnt and obeyed, but to be continually recited, lived in, and enjoyed: a sacrament, in fact, of communion. Our previous study of the wisdom books helps to explain this development. It appeared that the ancient sages had taught a disciplined 'way', a contemplative life in which the disciple grew ever closer to divine order and wisdom, and so to God himself. Some of their heirs in a later period came to expound this discipline of wisdom as devotion to the growing scriptures. For these circles the old contemplative way had gradually become the way of meditation in the Lord's *tora*. For them his statutes and ordinances had indeed become their wisdom; as their fathers had loved the constant yoke of wisdom, so they cherished *tora* in similar fashion.

Psalms like chains of proverbs

There are several psalms which resemble little collections of proverbs. They have the style of teaching addressed to disciples and use thoughts and phrases typical of the wisdom books. Compositional shape and unity are achieved by following the letters of the alphabet in the initial letters of the sections, and also by moving in and around one broad theme.

The longest of these is Psalm 37. Each section beginning with its due letter of the Hebrew alphabet has two verses, each with two parts, for example (Letter B):

> Be trusting in the Lord and do good,
>> abide in the land and feed on faithfulness,
> and delight in the Lord,
>> and he will give you the requests of your heart.
>
> 37.3–4

The broad theme in this psalm is the counsel of trust in the Lord in a situation of affliction and provocation. The disciple is urged not to envy the apparent success of unscrupulous oppressors, but to hold to the good way, rejoicing in the fellowship of God and waiting trustfully for the full disclosure of his plans.

There are several close resemblances to the contemplative teaching we discovered in the wisdom books. Here again the life of discipline and restraint is valued. In the right way of life 'a little' is ample, and more beneficial than abundant wealth of the wicked (Ps. 37.16). Rather than roving with ambition and greed, it is better to abide in one's place, enjoying faithful relationships, finding fulfilment of all desire in the knowledge of God (37.3–4, translated above).

And here again we have praise of humility and denunciation of arrogance. The humble will possess God's land and delight in his peace (37.11). By contrast the sage recounts how he saw an overbearing man grown great like a spreading tree; he looked and wondered; but when he came again the proud fellow had vanished, gone without trace (37.35–36). The style of the teaching here, as a personal experience, reminds us of that of the warning against idleness in Proverbs 24.30–34: 'I passed by . . . I saw and considered . . .'.

The psalmist speaks personally also about God's care:

> I was a boy and now am an old man,
> and I have not seen a true person forsaken
> and his children searching for bread . . .

This line of teaching rather lends itself to abuse, as Job found to his cost. The psalmist's intention, however, is to give expression to the genuine and wonderful experience of God's care and so to encourage the disciple in a time of need and oppression.

We found in Proverbs how the limits of human knowledge are sometimes indicated by contrasting the careful plans of man with the actual outcome decreed by the mysterious decisions of God (Prov. 19.2; 20.24). For our psalmist also, the steps of a person are from the Lord; he makes firm the one whose way delights him; falls he will have, but the Lord will take him up (Ps. 37.23–24).

Again, we found that silence and quietness were prized by the sages as suitable for one recognizing the decisive power of God. How well the psalmist expresses this God-ward quietness and patience:

> Be still to the Lord
> and wait in hope for him!
>
> 37.7

Then there is the divine giving. The good things come as God's gift, not as grasped by human desire. As desire and delight are fixed on him, all needs are met by his bountiful giving (v. 4). It is he who will vindicate the faithful oppressed, he who will cause them to inherit the earth (37.6, 9). In him they find all fulness.

Committing his purposes to the Lord, the disciple finds God acting in them. Here the image of 'rolling', which we met in Proverbs 16.3, occurs again; it perhaps pictures the rolling out of a scroll of plans, or even a roll of material in the market, for approval:

> Roll out your way before the Lord
> and trust in him and he himself will perform it.
>
> 37.5

Trust in the Lord is basic (vv. 3, 5), and makes possible the quiet 'waiting' which is enjoined repeatedly (vv. 7, 9, 34). Such waiting is essential to all meditation, and goes with a steadfast keeping to the Lord's way (v. 34), undistracted by anger at the seeming triumphs of the wicked.

There are various expressions of close communion in the psalm. The disciple is to enter the embrace of God as a fortress; he takes refuge 'in him' (vv. 39–40). He delights in the Lord (v. 4), is still to him (v. 7). And the Lord reciprocates, 'knowing his days' (v. 18) – being with him in all his daily round – and delighting in his way (v. 23). The communion also seems to take the form we found in Psalms 1 and 119: recital of the divine teachings, refreshing heart and soul in the divine will:

> The mouth of the true person meditates wisdom
> and his tongue speaks justice,
> in his heart is the teaching (*tora*) of his God,
> his steps do not slip.
>
> 37.30–31

It is interesting to notice here the unity of thought regarding 'wisdom', 'justice/order', and God's *tora*. The mouth expresses what is in the heart, and the exercise of vocal meditation strengthens and perfects the whole being in the way of harmony with God.

The alphabetic method of composition, so suitable for

memory and meditation, is used more concisely in Psalms
111 and 112. For each successive letter there is the shortest
possible unit beginning with that letter – a half-verse. There
are familiar wisdom teachings: the beginning and chief part
of wisdom is the fear of the Lord (111.10), the true person
has well-being and is encouraging and generous to all
around him (112.1–9), the wicked end in nothingness
(112.10).

Especially interesting in these two psalms is the use of
wisdom style in thanksgiving. Since the teaching declares in
effect the way God works in human life, it can become a
testimony and praise to him. Psalm 112 shows something of
this use in that it is prefaced with the call to praise: 'Halleluia!'
Psalm 111 has this also, but is itself more obviously an
expression of thankful praise in a company of worshippers
(111.1). Most of this psalm declares his power and grace to
those who fear him and to his covenanted people (111.5, 9).
Such combination of wisdom tradition with themes of covenant and law (111.7) in an assembly gathered for praise
indicates the circles and practices which eventually give us
Ben Sira and his school. The study of the sacred records, that
creative dialogue with tradition which blossomed in the
rabbinical world of the Sayings of the Fathers, may already be
referred to in 111.2:

> Great are the deeds of the Lord,
> studied by all who delight in them.

These two little alphabetic psalms complement each other
well, the first portraying God in his gracious works, and the
second the disciple who fears this God and hence possesses
and spreads blessing. The psalmist-sage gathers his whole
group into the contemplation of God and the life which is ever
marked by that contemplation.

A still smaller proverb-chain, not alphabetic, is formed by
Psalm 127. This shares the typical contemplative view of work
and gifts:

> If the Lord himself does not build the house,
>   in vain its builders labour on it.
> If the Lord himself does not guard the city,
>   in vain the guard keeps vigil.

> It is all in vain, you who are anxious to rise early
>   and go late to rest,
>   you who eat the bread of toil –
> so he gives his beloved one sleep!

What a view of work! As you cut the beams and lay the stones, the Lord himself is doing the work if you are open to him. As you are vigilant in your duties, he is on guard with you. As you grow your crop, it is he who must do it. Knowing that the success of the work is his achievement and his gift, you are at peace, relaxed. Trusting in his love, you sleep like a child.

It has been said of Chinese philosophy that it is all about how to 'fall asleep' rather than to 'take a nap', accepting the gift rather than distrustingly grasping.[10] This is the spirit of our psalm. It goes on to illustrate the thought with the gift that ancient families so highly desired: the birth of numerous sons. By them the family would become strong, respected in the disputes of the judicial gatherings in the gateway. It would be readily recognized that such a family could not be procured at human command, but came mysteriously by God's appointment.

The psalm's title 'Of Solomon' seems not have been known by the Greek translators around 200 BC, and may be an addition suggested by the psalm's content, the 'house' being understood as the temple built by Solomon, the Lord's 'beloved'. The psalm is in the series of 'psalms of the steps' (so the titles of Pss. 120–134) and may have been sung on a processional ascent in the great festivals. It would then respond to the desires of the worshippers for the great 'house of the Lord', his holy 'city', the opening year of growth ('bread') and the need of fertility ('sons').

Thus the little psalm is of special interest in showing a moment when the contemplative spirit of the sages is offered to the national multitudes in their concern for the replenishment of their life and livelihoods. Some modern states might have used the opportunity to teach the merit of heroic toil and of will-power dedicated to the achievement of growth targets and productivity. But these ancient worshippers were given a song about 'falling asleep', relaxing as a trustful child in the divine arms.

The theme is well represented in the French poems of Charles Péguy (1873–1914). 'O Night,' God says, 'you obtain sometimes the most difficult thing in the world . . . the resignation of man into my hands . . . for his ideas to be still and no longer shake about in his head like seeds in a pumpkin . . . I do not like the man who does not sleep. . . . The one who pleases me . . . rests in my arms like a laughing baby, (who) sees the world in its mother's eyes . . . only sees it and looks at it there.'[11]

Wisdom, praise and contemplation

Teaching in the wisdom style appears in other psalms where an assembly of worshippers seems to be present. Psalm 32 resembles the psalms of thanksgiving, where a singer thanks God in the temple for a particular deliverance and gives a testimony about his former trouble, his cry to God, and God's answering action (for example, Psalms 30, 116, 138). But the weight in Psalm 32 falls on the counsel which the singer gives on the basis of his own case. He declares as happy indeed the one who, having turned to the Lord with frank confession of sin, has received forgiveness. He recounts his own exemplary case. Refusing to acknowledge his sin, he suffered continually: 'By day and by night your hand was heavy upon me.' But when he made confession to the Lord, he was forgiven and restored. He found a refuge in the Lord. Trusting in him, he was surrounded by his faithful love.

Explicitly he draws the lesson (32.6): therefore let every faithful soul in trouble pray to God, pray, that is, with earnestness, frankness and trust. The counsel is developed with special force in verses 8–9. Some have thought that the singer here is passing on directly a word he received from the Lord, 'I' being God himself. But as this is not expressly indicated and is not really to be expected at this point in the psalm's structure, it is better to understand the 'I' as the singer himself. The situation would be like the *tawajjuh* of the Sufis, a total face-to-face attention in which the master may concentrate on his disciple to enter deeply into his soul and guide him.[12] How solemnly then the psalmist gives sagely counsel, how earnest his gaze, and how forcefully he uses his image from the animal world:

> I will give you insight
> and guide you in the way you should go,
> let me counsel you,
> my eye set upon you.
> Don't be like a horse,
> a mule with no understanding,
> whose course must be checked with bit and bridle
> or he will not keep with you.
>
> 32.8–9

The way commended is one of trust. The disciple is to be open to God, responsive to his guidance, without needing severe constraint. The final call to the group for praise appropriately starts, 'Rejoice in the Lord'. The true person is united with God in trust and in joy.

Similar elements make up Psalm 34, which furthermore assists meditation by running through the alphabet with the initial letters of its verses. The singer is full of thanksgiving and praise, and he calls on all the gathering, ideally pictured as 'the humble', to join in:

> I will bless the Lord at every (set) time,
> his praise shall be duly in my mouth.
> Let my soul swell with praise for the Lord,
> let the humble hear my story and rejoice.
> With me declare how great is the Lord,
> together let us raise his name on high.
>
> 34.1–3

The singer then tells briefly how he had sought the Lord and been answered and delivered from all his fears (34.4, 6). For the rest, sixteen verses are devoted to the lesson all should learn from this, set out in the manner of proverbs. The role of the sage-like teacher towards his disciples is made quite clear:

> Come, children, and listen to me.
> The fear of the Lord I will teach you.
>
> 34.11

Of several striking sayings in this teaching perhaps the most remarkable is the bold summons:

> Taste and see that the Lord is good!
> Happy the person who shelters in him!
>
> 34.8

With this we may compare verse 5:

> Contemplate him and be radiant
> and your faces shall not be abashed!

With such verses it is not surprising that in church use the psalm has been especially associated with the eucharist, and is often quoted by Christian mystics. With the language of feeding and seeing, a contact with God is indeed suggested, giving as it were a sweet taste in the soul and a face that shines with reflection of the divine appearing. A poem of Kabir comes to mind:

> Taste it,
> This love
> O Kabir.
> Without its taste
> One understands
> Nothing![13]

In our previous study of the theme of the knowledge of God in the wisdom books, we made a connection between the sages' teaching of 'the fear of the Lord' and their awesome experience of God. We may make a similar connection in this psalm. 'The fear of the Lord' is a main theme (34.7, 9, 11) and can well be taken here to refer to a life coloured throughout by moments of contact with God. The disciple will 'seek the Lord' (v. 4), find him 'near' (v. 18), 'shelter in him' (vv. 8, 22), 'contemplate' him (v. 5), 'taste and see that he is good' (v. 8). With such knowledge of God, he lives in constant awareness of him – in the 'fear' of him; he does good and avoids evil, and he diligently seeks what is wholesome (vv. 13–14).

The contradictions of experience

Just as the wisdom books, especially Job and Ecclesiastes, showed us how the best traditions of teaching could be battered on the rocks of experience, so there are wisdom psalms which arise from a severe crisis for faith. In Psalm 73 we meet someone who almost lost his footing on the steep path of wisdom. Wicked and arrogant people were defying God's laws with impunity. Lusty and oppressive, they lived in ease. What was the use of his efforts for purity and innocence when his own lot was daily suffering? But he was restrained from openly declaring the futility of faithfulness by the thought of his obligation to God's 'children'.

In perplexity he went into God's sanctuary, and there was given insight into the illusory character of the success of the wicked. He saw that he had been stupid to be bitter. For in God he had all that was worthwhile. He was continually with God, who grasped his right hand. God would ever guide him with his counsel and one day receive him in glory. Though heart and flesh failed, God would ever be his strength and portion. To be far from God was to perish, but, helped by the ministries of the temple, he had come near to God and found the supreme good. Having found refuge in God, his work was now to bear witness to him.

At first sight this all seems to be another case of a thanksgiving with story of deliverance and a lesson for a gathering of worshippers. Its special interest for us would be the role of the sanctuary as the place where insight was given and where God was known in wonderful closeness.

But on further inspection we notice that explicit address in the psalm is always to God and never to companions (73.18–28). Also we observe that the scandal of the prosperity of the oppressors is aired eloquently and at length. So the psalm begins to appear rather as a meditative *prayer*. The vexatious situation is held fully before God, along with persuasive statements of confidence in his justice and in his intimate love, and an undertaking to bear witness to his eventual intervention. If this is a truer description of the nature and aim of the psalm, it still remains that the statements of confidence and intimacy are very remarkable:

> My heart was growing bitter,
>   I felt a gnawing in my kidneys,
> for I was stupid and could not understand,
>   I was like a beast towards you.
> But now I am ever beside you,
>   you hold me by my right hand.

> By your counsel you guide me
>> and at last you will take me into glory.
> Whom do I need in heaven?
>> Beside you I want no one on earth.
> My heart and my flesh fail –
>> rock of my heart and my portion is God for ever!
>> 73.21–26

It is not certain that the psalmist here is thinking of a glory after death. This would not be a typical Old Testament hope, though gleams of it may be found in the Psalms, originating perhaps in ideas about the king as the special intimate of God (e.g. 21.4f.). What the psalm clearly and warmly expresses is a present experience of God, which outweighs all tribulations. Here is the supreme good; and time and even death are as nothing in comparison. In this way the psalm reminds us of Job, where also the triumph over suffering was won in the immediacy of God's presence.

Meditation in a time of crisis is illustrated also by Psalm 77. Judging from the whole course of this psalm, the crisis appears to be suffered by the community. The singer is a representative figure, but his personal style of utterance tells us something of the meditative approach to suffering.

The opening account of grieving prayer centres on 'seeking the Lord':

> My voice is for God and I cry aloud,
> my voice is for God and he will give ear to me.
> In the day of my trouble I have sought the Lord,
> through the night my hand is stretched out and does
>> not weary,
> my soul refuses to be consoled.
> I call the name of God with ceaseless murmur,
> I meditate and my spirit grows faint.
>> 77.1–3

A reference to 'my music' suggests the accompaniment of lyre or harp:

>> I recite (with) my music in the night,
>> I meditate with my heart
>> and my spirit delves deep.
>> 77.6

He addresses to God recitals of his mighty works of old. Here is enclosed a strong prayer that the mysterious God, moving with unseen footprints (v. 19), will yet again lead the way from bondage. These recitals are also seen as the stuff of meditation:

> I will recite the deeds of the Lord,
> yes, I will recite your marvels of old.
> I will intone the story of your work
> and your deeds I will utter in meditation.
>
> 77.11f.

A clear example of the use of the lyre in meditation is found in Psalm 49. Facing the problem of the tyranny of the rich and powerful, the singer opens up the dark puzzle with his lyre. Having thus received the illumination of 'wisdom', he can now convey through music his proverb-like teaching (49.1–4). The message of the psalm is disputed. As with Psalm 73, there is a question of whether life after death is envisaged. While 'Death' is the grim minder of those who trust in their pomp and wealth, the psalmist apparently has a better hope:

> But God will ransom my soul
> from the hand of the Underworld,
> yes, he will take me.
>
> 49.15

Is this again a taking into 'glory' – heavenly glory? At all events there is further evidence here of a strong experience of communion with God among psalmists who had some links with wisdom teaching. For the possible thought of eternity we could compare ancient Egyptian wisdom teaching. This warns against trust in earth's passing goods and commends humble and righteous ways that would bring eternal benefit:

> Do not trust in length of years, for they (the gods) regard a lifetime as but an hour. A man remains over after death and his deeds are placed beside him in heaps.[14]

> A single day gives for eternity
> and an hour gives beauty for futurity.[15]

Beholding the divine beauty

A number of psalms which have fine expressions of experience of God may well have been intended as prayers of the king, though this is disputed. Among other near eastern peoples we find the tenderest expressions of knowledge of the deity in the mouth of kings. Thus Assyrian monarchs speak of their god who spreads his shadow over them. A Hittite king tells of taking refuge with his god as a bird shelters in its nest. Reliefs show such a king as walking closely with his god; his head nestles in the shoulder of the god, whose arm passes round the king's neck and upholds his hand by clasping his wrist.[16] Such instances could be multiplied.

According to Israelite royal ideals, the king was taken into a son-like intimacy with God in order to mediate the blessings of God's kingship to the world. The psalmists would therefore depict the relationship with outstanding colour and imagery. They would no doubt be drawing on their own intimations of communion with God, and they were fashioning ideals which would come to inspire all who longed for God.

In Psalms 61 and 63 the king mentioned can naturally be taken to be the person praying in the entire psalm. The harsh note of 63.9–10 thus falls into place. The king's enemies are to fall on the battlefield and so be prey to the foxes. Before the battle is joined, the king approaches God in the sanctuary, confessing his need and seeking replenishment:

> O God, you are my God,
> I seek you earnestly.
> My soul thirsts for you,
> my flesh pines for you
> in a parched and weary land without water.
> So in the sanctuary I look for you
> to see your power and your glory.
> For your faithful love
> is better than life itself . . .
> My soul shall be satisfied as with rich fare,
> with joyful lips my mouth will give praise,
> as I recite your name upon my bed
> and meditate on you in the watches of the night.

> For you are my deliverance
> and in the shadow of your wings I will rejoice.
> My soul cleaves to you,
> your right hand takes hold of me.
>
> 63.1–8

What a remarkable string of mystical statements! The contemplation of God is associated here with the sanctuary, meditative recital through the night, hunger and thirst that will be richly satisfied, nestling under the divine wings, cleaving to God, being held by his hand.

The sanctuary ('tent') and the divine wings recur in Psalm 61, where there is also emphasis on the image of refuge:

> Lead me on to the rock that is high above me,
> for you are my refuge, a stronghold against the enemy.
> I will dwell in your tent for ever,
> I will shelter in the cover of your wings.
>
> 61.2–4

Between these two psalms lies Psalm 62 with its emphasis on trusting and waiting before this God of refuge. In a time of danger appeal is made to God indirectly by declarations of trust and exhortations to the people to trust likewise:

> To God my soul is still,
> from him comes my salvation . . .
> Yes, to God be still, my soul,
> for from him comes my hope . . .
> Trust in him at all times, O people,
> pour out your heart before him!
> God is our refuge.
>
> 62.1, 5, 8

Striking expression of contemplation occurs also in another psalm that could well be a king's prayer, Psalm 27. However terrible the foes that mass against him, he trusts the Lord to exalt him in victory. His hope is for a continuing life close to the God who reveals his will and presence in the sanctuary:

> The Lord is my light and my salvation.
>   Whom then shall I fear? . . .
> One thing have I asked of the Lord,
>   that alone I seek,

> that I should sit in the house of the Lord
> all the days of my life,
> to behold the beauty of the Lord
> and enquire his will in his temple.
>
> 27.1, 4

Another psalm outstanding for its personal sense of God, 139, has also been understood by some scholars as the prayer of a king. Again a harsh note then falls into place: in claiming to hate the wicked with perfect hatred (v. 21), he means to say that he has no part with them but wholly stands for right as God's ruler should. He prepares for his prayer for help with a long meditation on how God knows him intimately and to the roots of his being. God knows his every word and thought. Behind and before he encloses him and rests his hand upon him. As embryo he was woven by God's hand in the darkness and his days were already allotted. Let this God now search him and see where the fault lies between him and his foes!

In such psalms, then, we seem to meet kings whose life is greatly at risk from martial foes and traitors, and who seek safety in the intimate protection of the God who has called them to their task.[17] Thus some of the Psalter's richest expressions of contemplation seem to be associated with the responsibilities of rule and what we call 'politics'. This is in harmony with our findings in the wisdom books. It is not one cut off from the world who pines for vision in the sanctuary, meditates through the night, sits still before the Lord and shelters under his wings. It is in keeping with this that in face of international tumult the peoples are called to a contemplative way:

> Be still
> and know that I am God.
>
> 46.10

Thirsting for God and seeing his face

The enmity of an 'unfaithful nation' weighs upon the singer of Psalms 42–43 (one psalm in two phases), and so prompts one of the outstanding images of yearning for God. It is the image of a fallow-deer, probably the gentle doe. She wanders in a drought-stricken land, stretching for the scent of water as though imploring her Creator for aid (cf. Joel 1.20). So the psalmist thirsts for God:

> As a deer pants for channels of water,
> so my soul pants for you, O God.
> My soul thirsts for God, the living God.
> When shall I enter and see the face of God?
>
> 42.1–2

He recalls the happy time when he had led the dancing procession into the house of God, so clearly the vision that he longs for is such as was given him in the sanctuary. In the refrain, which occurs three times, he bids his mourning soul to 'hope' in God and to wait trustingly.

The expression 'to see the face of God' was modified in later pronunciation to mean 'to appear before the face of God'. It occurs in a number of passages as the goal of all pilgrims to the sanctuary (Exod. 23.15; 34.20, 23–24; Deut. 16.16; 31.11; I Sam. 1.22; Isa. 1.12). Our psalmist likewise is referring to a hoped-for completion of pilgrimage, when he will reach God's holy hill and dwelling and approach the altar and offer a song of praise (43.3–4).

His thirst for God is also a conception applicable to pilgrims generally. The singer of Psalm 84 probably represents the ideal for all arriving at the festival:

> How lovely your abode, Lord of hosts!
> My soul pined and fainted for the courts of the Lord,
> my heart, my whole body cried out for the living God.
> Now my soul is a bird that has found its home,
> a swallow building a nest to lay her young
> close to your altars, Lord of hosts,
> my King and my God.
>
> 84.1–3

Such rich experience is an ideal not only for all Israel; according to Psalm 36 it is a universal gift:

> In the shadow of your wings mankind shelters,
> they feast on the goodness of your house,
> you give them drink from your delicious streams.
> Beside you rises the fountain of life
> and in your light we see light.
>
> 36.7–9

Such psalms, then, witness to the ancient invitation to all pilgrims to an encounter with God to worship which would be a replenishment of life: bestowal of the light and water of life. The encounter is expressed in striking terms. That the phrase 'to see the face of God' was modified by later users of the texts agrees with the sense of awe, indeed terror, which is uppermost in other Old Testament contexts. The stories of Moses illustrate the varying views. Sometimes he is said to have met God 'face to face' (Deut. 34.10; Exod. 33.11; 34.29f.), 'mouth to mouth' and 'seeing the form of the Lord' (Num. 12.6–7). But another passage relates how he can only be granted a restricted view of the divine glory (Exod. 33.18f.). Again, there are passages where the people or a group of elders come face to face with God (Deut. 5.11; Num. 14.14; Exod. 24.10f.), but other accounts reveal fear of death from seeing God (Judg. 6.22; Isa. 6.5).

The Old Testament texts thus witness to two sides of the direct experience of God. He is holy and terrible, overwhelming to mortal creatures; who can endure when he appears? But there is also a revelation that he stoops to give in love, a revelation of unspeakable beauty, bestowing the fullness of life.

The living species in God's hand

The ancient wisdom schools liked to order knowledge by grouping comparable things or compiling lists. From Egypt we have, for example, a list of all that the Creator (Ptah) first made in heaven and on earth.[18] The order of the items sometimes resembles that of God's works surveyed in Job 38–39. Psalm 104 also surveys the 'manifold creatures' of God and has some kinship with Egyptian compositions. In reflecting on God and his world without reference to Israel, the psalm is in harmony with Proverbs and Job. Moreover the psalm states that the Lord made his manifold creatures through 'Wisdom' (v. 24). The link with the meditative psalms is evident in the psalm's being expressed as praise of a single person before God, and also in the description of it as a 'meditation' sent up to him as an offering (v. 34).

The nearest Egyptian composition is the Hymn to the Aton.[19] This expresses meditative praise of the Creator manifest in the sun; it is a meditation of one who knows him in his heart, one who alone truly knows him – a meditation of the king Akh-en-aton. It dwells on the beauty with which God shines into the world and on the life and joy he brings to all creatures at his daily rising: to trees, plants, birds, fish, cattle, wild animals, all peoples, cities, fields, roads, and the great river. There is special wonder at the divine working in secret, beyond the knowledge of men. God soothes the child in the dark womb, a constant nurse. Marvellously he gives breath to the chick in the shell, so that it can breathe and speak. He enables the chick to come out at its appointed time, speaking and walking on its legs. For all the animals and all the nations he cares and provides. He himself is their 'lifetime' – they live only through him.

The single figure meditating in Psalm 104 prepares for a prayer against the earth's wrong-doers (v. 35). Perhaps he too is a king, regarded as called to special intimacy with the Creator, responsible for mediating knowledge of him and for good order in the realm. He begins his praise with reference to the bright glory of the Creator, supreme over the great cosmic elements. The founding of the earth and the masterful disposing of the waters are subjects of wonder. All has been done for joyful life. Springs gush in the valleys and refresh the wild creatures. Birds nest nearby and sing among the branches. From the rains come earth's many fruits, grass for the cattle and crops for man's cultivation. There is wine to cheer the heart and oil to make the skin shine and bread to give strength. Wonder rises at the thought of the great trees, 'the trees of the Lord', cedars of Lebanon and firs where storks nest.

There is a fitness in things: high crags for the wild goats, rocky slopes for the holes of badgers. Moon and sun know their allotted task. Night also serves the Lord and is the proper time of lions, who roar and seek their food from God. It is the proper time for human rest, as the day is the time for work. The fullness of creature life cannot be told, and all is made by God through Wisdom. The sea itself is a miracle, teeming with hidden life, small and great, a place for the ships and for the monster Leviathan, now subdued and even playful before God. All look to God, all depend on him. All live by the attention of his face, the opening of his hand, the outbreathing

of his breath. There comes a time when he withholds his face
and breath; then the creatures die and return to the earth.
When he sends his breath again, there is renewal. God is
terrible: earth trembles under his gaze, mountains smoke at
his touch. But he rejoices in his creative and caring work, and
the singer's meditation is offered up to please him.

Our poet is caught up in a contemplative view of the world,
sensing its unity in the life-giving care of God. The unspeakable multitude of God's creatures are at one in depending on
him and witnessing to his wisdom, power and goodness.
Appropriately the main meditation has begun with vision of
his greatness and beauty and ends with his glory and joy in
creation and his dread-inspiring holiness. There is indeed a
similarity with the climax of the Book of Job (38–42), where
God discloses himself in the wonder of his world, a God of
wisdom, beauty and care; terrible, yet bringing peace and
renewal.

Reflecting on our psalms

We have been exploring wisdom and contemplation in the
Psalms. On the way we have sampled a variety of fine poems
of the spiritual life. To what extent can we trace their
relationships to the wisdom books and to each other?

Several considerations would lead us to expect contacts
between the sages and the temple singers. Both have a royal
patron, David for the psalmists and Solomon for the sages.
Moreover, Solomon the supreme sage was also builder of the
temple. Both sages and psalmists inherited tradition from
Egyptian and other near eastern culture. Both worked in
poetry. Both needed scribal skills to collect their materials
through the centuries into our present books. All in all, it is not
wholly surprising that there are psalms quite similar to the
wisdom books in thought and expression, psalms which may
be early (Ps. 104), late (49), or somewhere in between (32, 34,
37, 112, 127). In these poems we found many marks of the
contemplative life: the sense of universal order under the
caring hand of God; the turning from anxiety, jealousy and
ambition to acceptance of his gifts; trust in his grace; discipline; and the way of knowledge of God – a tasting, a

beholding, which fills all moments of life with awe and awareness of his power and care.

Then we found some psalms which were still akin to the old wisdom literature but distinct from it in an important respect: they show the temple as the place of awesome encounter with God. This feature is understandable in the light of the psalmists' task of voicing prayer and praise in the Jerusalem temple. The temple was their sphere. It fell to them to express its meaning and value in words.

And again the connecting threads led to the king. There were signs that these psalms developed their imagery of vivid meeting with God from the ideals of the king, the Lord's Anointed, who was called to know him and be close at his side as a beloved son (Pss. 27; 61–63; 91). At the same time the psalmists would express experience of God in his holy place which they also knew in their life of musical service and contemplation, and which all devout pilgrims could share (8; 42–43; 84). In a world of dangerous foes, oppression and injustice, the seeker could draw near in God's 'house', quieten his heart in trustful meditation (63; 139) and be replenished in soul and vision (63; 73; 84). Here before God, drinking deep of the fountain of life, illumined by divine light, the worshipper could have a fulfilment which overcame all terrors, even death itself (63.2; 73.23f.).

Such encounter with God in his sanctuary is not a theme occurring in the main wisdom books. It is the special focus of the psalmists in their particular calling. But in the psalms which express this theme we still find threads connecting with the wisdom tradition. There is the development of contemplation from wonder at the natural order (Ps. 8) and from the marvels of one's own createdness (139). There are the counsels of quietness and trust (62). And there is a long treatment of the contradictions of divine justice in society, a Job-like theme, resolved in meeting with God (73).

Then there were other psalms, again akin to the wisdom books, but distinctive in another respect: for them God is known especially in devotion to his *tora* and commandments. Here there is much teaching of the good 'way' (Pss. 1, 119). As in the wisdom books, it is a way which parts sharply from that of the 'scoffers', the proud and the wicked. It is a way of truth and humility, of seeking God with the whole heart. But it is particularly the way of meditating in his *tora*, taking delight in his words of guidance and command, nourishing the depths of the soul by finding his presence continually in the recitation of his name and teachings. Contemplation again develops from attention to nature – stars and rising sun (Ps. 19), but even these great elements are sensed as sharing in the universal work of knowing God in recitation of his acts and in obedience; they are signs of the glorious, restoring, saving, life-giving power which God sends out in his teaching and commands. The remembrance of the deeds of God, the glad reception of his guiding words – this is to meet the Creator and to have true life in his presence.

Such centring of communion in *tora* meditation reminds us of our later examples of wisdom literature, Ecclesiasticus and the Sayings of the Fathers. But it has some old roots. Around the sixth century BC circles connected with Deuteronomy considered true wisdom to be the keeping of the Lord's ordinances (Deut. 4.5f.). They pictured the ideal king (17.18f.), the leader Joshua (Josh. 1.8) and King Josiah (II Kings 23) as devoted to God's *tora* and covenant. In all this they may well have been developing ancient ideals of royal piety. It would therefore be unwise to treat the *tora*-piety of these psalms as purely a late development, even though it is not found in the old wisdom books. But it came to have a particular importance as the scriptures developed with a central role in Jewish religious life. It was to constitute one of the great forms of Jewish mysticism down to our own day.

In following a course of inquiry that has led us from the five Hebrew wisdom books to the Psalms, we have thus found both continuity and enrichment. The way of the sages is still apparent, a way for disciples, a cultivation of disciplined and pure living on a journey into knowledge of God, a contemplative way, a life of awe and delight in discovery of the divine reality. But in some psalms there further appears a rapture of knowing God in his sanctuary, while in yet other psalms the encounter beyond all other delights is given through meditation in the Lord's teaching or *tora*. For the main period of the psalmists the dominant theme is probably the revelation of God in the sanctuary. This is seen as central to the life of the world, the nation and the individual. In later times a great theme becomes his giving of himself to those who engage with the scriptures, eager for the sound of his voice. And in all periods the contemplative values of the old sages live on.

4

WISDOM CALLS TO THE MODERN WORLD

A new age of spiritual wisdom is coming to birth.

Bede Griffiths[1]

The way to the Truth is not that of progress but that of return.

Bede Griffiths[2]

The gates of an ancient oriental city, with their spaces and recesses and joinings of ways, were busy places. Donkeys and camels carry burdens for the villages. Porters sway past with high frames of boxes on their backs to penetrate into crowded alleys. Soldiers and officials, lawyers and money lenders, merchants and market women are busy here. Shrill voices offer wares, bargain passionately, threaten, and plead.

It was in such a concourse, not in the silence of the great open spaces, that the poet-sage of Proverbs 8 saw and heard Wisdom, the Thought of the Creator. She took her stand on a high place beside the way, where paths joined, at the great portals, at the mouth of the city, at the entrance of the gates – the phrases pile up to stress that precisely here, where people pursue their aims of getting and striving, here Wisdom raised her voice and called out and invited them to come to her for what was beyond price.

Where does she stand today? In a subway station at rush hour? In the stock exchange? In a big store on the first day of the sales? It will in any case be a place where people are

pitilessly absorbed in vain pursuits. And what does she say?
And if her invitation is heeded, where does she lead?

In this our final chapter we shall reconsider the themes and
meanings we have found in the sages and contemplatives and
relate them to the needs of our own time. We must not cast off
care for the ancient meaning in its own context, but in taking
the meaning up to test it against modern experience, we may
hope to enter into it more deeply, as well as to derive benefit
for modern living.

The offer of life

For many people today, the basic needs of physical existence
are amply met. For them especially, the search for meaningful
life becomes urgent. Hopes are pinned on sport, travel,
hobbies, arts, wealth, prestige, power. The amazing develop-
ments of technology appear to offer innumerable possibilities
for pleasure and recreation. New systems of communication
ensure that there is no dearth of advice, though much of it
comes from powerful profiteers.

The quest for life, for deeply satisfying, worthwhile life,
does not become correspondingly easier. The seekers indeed
seem the more distracted and confused. Could they perhaps
find help in the basic simplicities of the old sages?

Certainly the ancient invitation of Wisdom was to a discovery of 'life':

> Whoever finds me finds life . . .
> all who hate me love death.
>
> Prov. 8.35

She was 'the fountain of life'. The whole way we have traced
out, from discipline into the depths of love and the knowledge
of God, was 'the way of life'. And with the great positive
invitation went an exposure of false values. There was strong
warning to the young about the death-path of sexual licence.
Established citizens, turning their lust rather to prestige and
wealth, had much to learn from Qohelet, the monodrama of
the king who had everything and found it nothing – and then
began to find a better basis for life.

Wisdom's invitation to life is not addressed to a select circle but to the crowds and to those engrossed in the business of the world. And the life which she offers is not secluded from the breadth of human concerns. There is no hard-and-fast scheme about it. The individuals find their own manner of walking the way of awareness and truth. Some are kings or administrators, some parents, some traders, artists or farmers, some lifelong students, ascetics or philosophers. Wisdom can embrace and guide them all, according to their own vocations, and make them friends of God.

The contact with God is not restricted to special moments. From points of intensity, awareness towards the divine flows out into the whole current of the disciple's life. All that this person is and does, all work and rest and contemplation, comes to pass in the fear of the Lord, an open stillness to him. Such is the wholeness of life which Wisdom offers, a life which profoundly suits us, the life for which we are made.

Cosmic consciousness

The hope of the future would seem to lie with the small communities, sometimes associated with a larger community, which are springing up all over the world, consisting of men and women, married and single, seeking a new style of life which will be in harmony with nature and with the inner law of the Spirit.

Bede Griffiths[3]

Suddenly the down-to-earth practical people of today are worried about the accelerating devastation of the environment. A few facts and calculations reveal that pollution, destruction and exhaustion of earth's resources threaten to run out of control and beyond reversal. Nature, even for this ruthless generation, begins to appear less as a thing to be kicked, consumed and exploited, and more as a mother who may be fatally wounded and with whom we must die.

To this emergency the voice of Wisdom speaks. She speaks in accord with the witness of the world's contemplatives that we are part of a living whole. In this illumination nature is experienced not as a mere thing but 'as a living presence, infinitely good in its essence and finality'; this is to attain 'cosmic consciousness'.[4]

We have seen how Wisdom confirms the intuitions of a universal order expressed by poets, by ancient Egyptians, Chinese, Hindus, Buddhists. To see the unity of all in the divine spirit is to awaken from the nightmare of separation and heartless exploitation. To see eternity in things that pass away and infinity in finite things is to obtain pure knowledge. Not one tiny part or member of the universe can be treated with wanton cruelty without offence to the whole and damage to the perpetrator. The One in whom all subsists teaches that in as much as we do it to the least, we do it to him.

The Hebrew sages recognized the extraordinary achievements of human technology. It almost seemed as if there was nothing it could not hunt down and lay hold of, nothing in nature it could not master. And yet they warned that the essential would ever elude grasping, ruthless man. Wisdom, the Creator's thought and spirit that gives form and body to all existence, is known only to him. He contemplates her and communes with her, and allows only those to enjoy her who 'fear the Lord', who live in humility, awe and wonder. She is generous with gifts of technology, the sciences, arts and crafts. All these spring from her who is the first-born Thought, the divine skill, the Creator's creativity. But the gifts are for those who will take her way in love and reverence.

With her they can find again the joy of the world's beginnings, the primal and eternal delight in hills and waters, animals and plants. By care and contemplation of the manifold creatures, they become ready to see God and be utterly satisfied. As Job found, when all is seen with wonder – the unspeakable high processions of light and dark, the mysteries of rain and snow, the wise ways of the animals, the harnessing of primeval powers – then God may be seen and shattered lives remade.

The ecumenical spirit

Only an ecumenical movement among religions, each learning to accept and appreciate the truth and holiness to be found in the other religions, can answer the need of religion today.

Bede Griffiths[5]

After centuries of divisiveness, the ecumenical movement developed among twentieth-century Christians in search of unity in accordance with the Master's prayer 'that they may be one'. Meanwhile, events of the century led to vast migrations and minglings of populations, and so of cultures and religions. The ecumenic spirit, concerned with fellowship in the entire 'inhabited earth' (Greek *oikoumene ge*) has been stirred to extend the work of understanding and sympathy to other world religions. Without assertion or denial of competing claims, enriching progress has been made by the way of attention, humility and love.

Here we recognize a way like that of contemplative wisdom. And it is a striking fact that the fundamental tradition of Old Testament wisdom did not speak of the peculiar national forms of religion but of universal values. It was discourse in which the sages of other lands could readily join.

As the centuries passed, the rabbinical circles and the early Christians inherited the wisdom tradition and joined it with their distinctive experiences of God. For the rabbis it illuminated the divine presence in the sanctuary of Jerusalem and in the study of *tora*. For the Christians it served to express the divine manifestation in Christ, the Word become flesh.

But the universality of the old wisdom tradition retains its value, and the ecumenical task appropriate to our time can be encouraged by the figure of primal Wisdom. Her delight is with the whole race. Her address is to all peoples. Her teaching is in terms that all can respond to. Her mission is that of the Creator of all and reaches to all aspects of life. She who was born of God before anything was created calls to everyone, of whatever colour, culture or creed. All who heed and seek her will find her, a welcoming mother or bride. Her disciples are known by their atoning, forgiving ways and by their joy and trust. Their insignia are the faithful love and truth bound about their throats and written on the tablets of their hearts.

The mad scramble

Freed of the bonds of fear and desire, one begins to taste primordial, ontic freedom. Released into the present, one knows that intersection of time and eternity where reality is, where divinity dwells.

Philip Novak[6]

Was it the invention of the clock and the spread of watches? Was it the increase in reliance on pulsating machines or the introduction of the pocket diary? Was it the speeding up of travel or the invasion of the telephone? Was it the diet of factory food? Whatever it was that caused it, modern life is lived at a hectic pace. The traffic rushes and snarls. Businesses and universities look for quick returns. The days are crowded with engagements timed to the minute. Even entertainments are devised to compete with nerve-racking time limits. Word-games become 'count-downs'. Cricket, once a haven of contemplation, is made tense with limited overs and computerized calculations and records. Athletes, not content with competing in the race of the day, battle over split seconds with the record books. The young plug their precious ears with pounding electronic din that passes for music. Characters become hyperactive, nervous, jerky and unreflective. Few have time or patience to look at a painting or a tree long enough to find its soul. Few allow themselves deeply to enjoy their present task. And all this when inventions have saved us time from toil and increased the possibility of leisure.

Wisdom calls this hectic generation to attend to one thing at a time. She teaches a deep attention, with a heart willing to receive, quiet, turning from self. The gates are to be thrown open that the radiance of the eternal spirit may come in and make its home. Such a heart is not always out to control, but simply to enjoy. By such attention we escape the flame of separation and enter the harmony of the One. The listening person speaks for eternity and is satisfied with the presence of Wisdom, the mystery of God, without rushing to the ends of the earth.

Wisdom calls us to forsake the scramble of ambition. One attains nothing with the elbow. Rather should one ascend 'inwards', climbing the steps of humility to ever closer communion with the Lord. The greatest waters take the lowest place and there are near to Tao.

The Tao is mirrored only in a still pool. Wisdom teaches that

quietness befits those who are aware of God. Better than the
study of grammar is the study of silence. Why should one
speak much as if master of one's own destiny? The more
words, the more vanity. Be quick indeed to hear, but
deliberate in answering. The secret of the healing quietness is
its direction. We are to be 'still to the Lord', waiting upon him.

Wisdom would have us wait on God the giver of time and
times. The birth and the dying, the warring and the peace, the
time of every business under heaven is given in his mysterious
purpose. He has put a dimension of eternity in our hearts, a
great range of memory and hope, but not the power to
understand his work from first to last. So we walk by trust,
content with his purpose and his care that seeks again what is
driven away.

Wisdom has no part with laziness. Released from the strains
of ambition and anxiety, her people enjoy work in the rhythm
of the Creator's work. They create by reconciling the finite
with the infinite. In all their work they see God. Happy those
with time to study deeply the spiritual treasures of the past!
But honoured too are those whose physical labour is long and
exhausting, for they help to sustain the world and their prayer
is in their work.

To contemplate God and be radiant with his light it is not
necessary first to forsake all worldly duties. We have met a
king engulfed in war, who found his way in contemplation.
He looked for God in the sanctuary, seeking and waiting.
He yearned for God as the thirsty yearn for water. He recited the divine name and directed his heart to God through
the watches of the night. Thus his soul came to cling to the
Lord, and he felt the supporting grasp of God's right hand.
In times of national danger the whole people would be counselled to trust in God at all times, pouring out their heart
before him; and above all, to be still and know that he alone
is God.

The people today, however, will have a hard time of it with
the ruthless who would shape their souls. The hectic, grasping way of life is instilled by these shapers: the advertisers, the
packagers of news and views, the media, so pressurized
themselves. The people will need the counter-force of good
shapers, methods and patterns of meditation which persist-

ently guide the attention to the good and feed the soul upon truth. Wisdom, characteristically, does not force a system upon us. Some guidance there is in the praises of God which are common in the later wisdom books and psalms. And there are psalms which show how ordered patterns of words and thoughts were valued as leading the heart to delight with awe in God. But it remains our own task to find the focusing patterns, our mantras and mandalas, which can constantly shape our souls for God, countering the evil shapers. So we will learn again to work and rest, live and play with a deep inner tranquillity. Fish are happy in water, we shall say, and we in Tao.

The questioning of religious authority

The Sannyasi ('Renouncer') is one who is called to witness to this Truth of the Reality beyond the signs, to be a sign of that which is beyond signs.

Bede Griffiths[7]

In our time, claims for religious authority on the grounds of some heavenly decree have little credibility. Scriptures and popes, pundits and prophets have to establish their authority more by their fruits than their fiats. Our mixed cultures and world news systems ensure that every claimant to unique guardianship of truth is assessed in a context of many other claimants. Venerable institutions have to live with their record of past errors and misdemeanours which are widely known. Claims based on history are readily challenged, and it is the books and programmes undermining great claims which are most marketable.

To such an age the call of Wisdom is well suited. Here is no 'thus says the Lord' or even 'thus said Moses'. The characteristic appeal of Wisdom is to experience: taste and see! Go and watch the ant! Look upon the rainbow! The proverbs are not for unthinking acceptance, not for glib citation, but for deep consideration, deep in the body, and for sharpening the powers of discernment.

Wisdom calls us to look with full gaze at reality. From her disciples comes a Job who will not yield his honesty to avoid suffering. He will not pretend that his sufferings are a just retribution. He will not disguise the oppression of the poor and the worldly success of the wicked. He speaks as he sees: from out of the cities the victims groan and their prayers do not win relief.

Another disciple of Wisdom is Qohelet – another who preferred to feel the desolation and futility of life rather than be fed what is not truth. He sees the evil under the sun so clearly that he cries that it would be better to be dead, better still never to have been born and not to have seen the evil. When such a one can yet teach a way of joy, he has earned a hearing.

Wisdom and the modern goddesses

Modern science and technology are the fruit of the tree of the knowledge of good and evil. They are not evil in themselves, but they become evil when, as usually happens, they are separated from wisdom.

Bede Griffiths[8]

The ancient habit of personifying values as deities has not really died out. As modern goddesses, to whom praise and sacrifice are daily offered, we may instance Growth and Productivity, Science and Education. These last two have something in common with the ancient figure of Wisdom, for like her they are concerned with knowledge, training, skill and technology. Much faith has been reposed in them, and they have been looked to in every need.

In themselves, however, they have no power to guide or save, no true life in their own gift. Their worshippers, alas, are often motivated by the desire for power over rivals. Science is used for weaponry and ruthless profit, education for self-advancement and for mass mind-management.

Wisdom, too, will divulge secrets of nature. She also will offer to mend social relations and educate the individual to fulfilment of personal capacities. But she will not give powers unconditionally.

From first to last in her programme she is calling for a

dedicated life of response to eternal reality. Through all her teachings and promptings she is requiring a pattern of life lived with quiet and attentive awe before the Lord of the marvellous cosmic order. The one who would love her and be loved by her must accept the value of discipline and reproof, being weaned away from harmful tendencies, glad to be counselled by trusty and experienced guides of the soul, happy with little of worldly ease and wealth. Thus freed from the din of selfish desires, the seeker of Wisdom develops a wonderful faculty of attention, hearing and seeing, attuned to the divine reality everywhere present, humble, open, loving and forgiving. The quietness of the disciple is a response to the divine reality: how should one ever be talking and boasting when there is so much to be learnt and heard and seen?

Response to the great reality also involves modesty about our systems of thought and the ambition of our researches. To none has he given power to tell all the story of his works. Reaching the end of them, you are just beginning. If I say 'I will become wise', it proves far beyond me. Far is what is, deep, so deep – who can find it?

For all the disciple's work and effort, the givenness of the rewards is not forgotten. The great insights and discoveries, the exalting experiences are not felt to be gained by grasping, but come as delightful, surprising gifts.

Seekers of Wisdom's science and education must accept the pain of honesty. Here is the renunciation of comforting illusions, alluring attachments to what is less than good, to ways that are currently popular and profitable. The scientist or educators in Wisdom's way had best expect no credit as they do a work made pure in the fire of Wisdom. But they will be without jealousy, one in success and in failure, their work a holy sacrifice. This austere aspect is present from the outset. However attractive Wisdom is – and she is beautiful beyond all telling – her students must be prepared for the hardship of a long course of application and single-minded devotion. They must rise early to camp beside her wall. Sometimes her path seems tortuous. Heavy seem her fetters. As gold is tested in the fire, so those who seek pure knowledge are tried in the furnace of humiliation.

Wisdom and suffering

*Suffering arises because we are shut up in ourselves and experience
our own limitations. If we were surrendered to God, we would not
suffer. The physical pain might be there, even the mental pain, but
the soul in its depths, in its ground, would be at peace.*

Bede Griffiths[9]

The modern world has amply endured the range of sufferings
familiar to our race: wars and oppressions, catastrophes,
famine, disease and death. Some diseases have been overcome, but new ones have sprung up. International wars have
become rarer, but more devastating. Internal strife, manipu-
lated by outside powers, is the more rampant in many
countries with appalling results. Social disorders scar many
large cities.

The catastrophes of the twentieth century came when
hopes of progress to utopia were high. And in spite of all,
many still live in the hope that with more research disease can
be conquered; with more social planning communities can
cure violence; with more money and leisure individuals can
find happiness; with more organizations peoples can work
together in harmony.

Wisdom does not pour scorn on any effort for peace or
healing, relief or service. But she warns against illusory
expectations. All who come forward to serve the Lord must
prepare themselves for trials. The times appointed by the
mystery of divine purpose comprise times of death as well as
birth, killing as well as healing, weeping as well as laughing,
mourning as well as dancing, estrangement as well as
embracing, breakdown as well as rebuilding. And every
beauty under the sun has its time and then passes. To our
thinking it is an enigma. Though eternity is laid in our hearts,
we cannot envisage the whole work of God with his world
from beginning to end. To our mind it will often seem that all
is vanity, and the day of death better than the day of birth.

In all this, Wisdom teaches a sober realism and an ultimate
reliance on the One who is beyond our understanding but not
beyond our trust. Nor indeed beyond our heart-knowledge.

In relation with him is joy, over which the vanity and transience of things cannot prevail. There is joy in accepting from him gifts of light, or creative work, eating and drinking and seeing life with a beloved companion. In relation with him even the withering of this life can be borne. Indeed it serves to bring forward the essential. God's trusted love is found to be better than life itself. Then the sufferer's inexplicable words flow: I am ever beside you, you hold me by my right hand; by your counsel you guide me, and at the last you will take me into glory; you are all – whom else do I need? – heart and flesh fail but God is my portion for ever. Such words defy explanation, but they record an experience and invite the modern sufferer to explore their truth.

It is not an easy option. It involves all the devotion and self-surrender of the contemplative way, and it is no fleeing from responsibilities in the world. To the rulers and to the peoples Wisdom's counsel comes: Yes, to God be still, my soul, for from him come my hope; trust in him at all times, O people, pour out your heart before him; long to behold his beauty all the days of your life and to enquire his will; be still and know that I am God.

The oldest counsel and the best

That is why all love is holy, from the love of atoms or of insects to the love of man. It is always a reflection of the love of God.

Bede Griffiths[10]

No wisdom, science, philosophy or theology can take us further than love. Wisdom's call to the modern world is in the end a song of love. She calls passionately to our troubled generation that by love we heal our social wounds, by love we become good servants of the natural world, by love we find our true selves, and by love we know God and enter eternity. Here is the heart of the contemplative way, and the greatest mystery this way leads into is the knowledge that God himself is love.

Wisdom returns the love of her devotees. Like a mother or like a bride she embraces her dear one, the seeker of truth. She teaches faithful love, a sign to bind about the throat and write on the tablet of the heart. She teaches good-will towards adversaries: if one who hates you is hungry, give him bread. Show a love that goes beyond the exact rights of a case; pass over your injuries, cover with love your grievances. By love iniquity can be forgiven and cured, the presence of the Lord is known and evil departs. Do not repay harm with harm. So the Lord comes and bestows his blessing.

By what accident, by what mysterious guidance, by what hidden necessity did the Old Testament's collection of Solomonic wisdom writings come to include the Song of Songs? Here is no teaching sage, no mind-teasing proverb, no hymn, prayer or piety of law and sanctuary. But the Song is wisdom-like in its common humanity, its echoes of international poetry and its sympathetic knowledge of the natural world. What connection it has with Solomon is not clear. Some words have been thought to point to a much later date (fifth century BC or later), but it could have an ancestry in the singing at the royal court.[11]

More significant is the question as to when this song or cycle of songs came to bear a mystical meaning. To most scholars it has seemed that love here was simply the love of man and woman for each other, until first the Jewish, then the Christian traditions applied it to the love between God and people or, in the Christian view, Christ and his church or Christ and the soul.

The extraordinary veneration of some rabbis for the Song around New Testament times reflects a mystical interpretation, and this may conceivably go back some centuries. The contemplative aspect of the old wisdom tradition which we have traced would be fertile ground for the development of such an application. But in any case the mystical understanding of the Song rests on the contemplative insight that love is one. A beautiful expression of the relationship of lovers can thus become a fitting dialogue of love between the Lord and his people or disciple:

> The voice of my beloved!
> Behold, he comes leaping upon the mountains,
> skipping upon the hills.
> My beloved is like a roe or a young hart.

> See, he stands behind our wall,
> he looks in at the windows,
> peeping through the lattice.
>
> My beloved spoke and said to me,
> Rise up, my love, my fair one, and come away!
> For see, the winter is past,
> the rain is over and gone.

Song 2.8f.!

In tune with the spring-time the girl is full of thoughts of love. She imagines her hero bounding over the mountains like a gazelle, eager to find her. He comes to the wall of her house, peeps in at the apertures and calls her to rise and come away with him into the blossoming countryside. The heavy rain of winter has done its work. Now the sky is bright and the sun warm. The slopes are covered with new grass and colourful wild flowers. Her lover's voice is urging:

> The flowers appear on the earth,
> the time of the singing of birds is come,
> and the voice of the turtle-dove is heard in our land.
> The fig tree puts forth her green figs,
> and the vines in blossom give a good smell.
> Arise, my love, my fair one, and come away!

Song 2.12f.

The love song evokes the spirit of new awakening, spring after winter, in a harmony of love, flowers and joyful birds. The story of the lovers is not told out. Their yearning and delight are glimpsed in snatches of verse. But the snatches are part of the universal song of love and beauty and able to bear the rich mystical meaning which Origen, St Bernard of Clairvaux and many others have heard in them.

And it is right to have a song for this final good of the world, for love. The song is a glad thing, a beautiful, playful thing. When Wisdom, the Creator's first-born Thought, danced and played, delighting and giving delight in the dawn of time, did she not sing, and sing of love? Yes, Wisdom should begin and end with such a song.

The religions of today and their sages

Every religion has, therefore, to renew itself continually, to rediscover the hidden mystery to which it is intended to bear witness.

Bede Griffiths[12]

In each religion it is necessary to go back beyond its formulations, whether in scripture or tradition, to the original inspiration. . . . This hidden Source can only be found by those who follow the path of the traditional wisdom.

Bede Griffiths[13]

In calling to the modern world, Wisdom calls not least to its religions. The religions of today would do well to listen and learn from their contemplatives and from the long tradition we have traced behind them. The religions are not always disposed so to listen and learn. At times they have persecuted their own sages, even killed them. But again, in times of perplexity and institutional weakness, they have turned to them to benefit from their genuine first-hand experience of God.

The great organizations of religion today are troubled with tensions, doubts, dwindling support. From their contemplatives they can learn again of the one thing needful which may have been hidden by legalism, rationalism, organization, and many well-meant things which may have become obstacles. They can learn from them the way of Wisdom which leads deep into the knowledge of God.

For Christians, to take an example, the voice of Wisdom invites to refreshment of a fundamental experience: union with Christ the Logos, the Word or Thought of the Creator. Underlying the great New Testament expositions, such as John 1 and Colossians, is all the richness of the wisdom books which present the figure of first-born Wisdom. Enriching, too, are all the intuitions we have noted in other religions concerning the cosmic order, the divine life and reality, such as Maat, Brahman and Tao.

The Hebrew sages tell us of Wisdom who is the principle of all creation and of manifest reality. She is a revelation of world-meaning, giving entrance into knowledge of God. She is attested by witnesses who have bravely ascended the path of loving, single-minded dedication. She is apprehended by poets. And she is experienced as personal – one who meets us with delight, love and care. As Christians enter afresh into this heritage of witness to Wisdom, they can go beyond the shallowness and glibness with which the Incarnation is often presented today. Here is an invitation to the immense depths in the message that the Word became flesh; an invitation also to proclaim it afresh in terms of the profoundest intuitions of all the world's artists and lovers of truth.

Wisdom further reminds the religious organizations of the call to the individual, the invitation for the soul to take a guided path of ever closer relationship with the One. This is not to denigrate the modern emphasis on the community. But it is a reminder of the necessity of individual challenge, individual commitment and progress on the path into God, the path to the place where I alone must be united to God. Wisdom's way is characteristically taken by disciples one by one, glad of guidance from a spiritual counsellor. The disciple then receives tried and traditional guidance focused on individual need and forming a personal daily programme. All the truth the disciple enters is experienced at first hand. Between this individual programme and the full community of worshippers are smaller circles, where the disciples share in praise and meditation under their sage's guidance.

And beyond the full community is the universal order. Wisdom will not let the religions close out the air and spaces, the great lights and darks and deeps, the myriad creatures which like us are in the hand of God. So Wisdom calls to the great religions, makes disciples one by one, takes them each on a personal pilgrimage, not to end in isolation but in the communion of infinite love. The religions do well to value their contemplatives, for they are friends of God, infecting others with the love of God, and benefactors of all creation.

Notes

1 Meeting the Sources

1. Kumar, *The Vision of Kabir*, p. 91.
2. Outstandingly von Rad, *Wisdom in Israel*. For orientation and bibliography useful works are: J. A. Emerton, 'Wisdom', in G. W. Anderson (ed.), *Tradition and Interpretation*; Bergant, *What Are They Saying About Wisdom Literature?*; and Crenshaw, *Old Testament Wisdom, An Introduction*.
3. My *Job*, pp. 39–41.
4. My *Job*, pp. 52–62.
5. My *Job*, p. 29.
6. As note 4.
7. A translation is given by Danby, *The Mishnah*; text, translation and commentary in Herford, *The Ethics of the Talmud*.
8. Pritchard (ed.), *Ancient Near Eastern Texts*, p. 412.
9. After Pritchard, p. 412.
10. For the sources of the following points on Maat see Helck (ed.), *Lexikon der Ägyptologie* III, cols. 110f.
11. So Schwartz, *The World of Thought in Ancient China*, pp. 121f.
12. Lau, *Lao Tzu: Tao Te Ching*.
13. Schwartz, p. 192.
14. Schwartz, pp. 211f.
15. Louth, *The Origins of the Christian Mystical Tradition*, pp. 1f.
16. Louth, pp. 19f.
17. Louth, pp. 36f.
18. S. Tugwell in Jones (ed.), *The Study of Spirituality*, p. 108.
19. Louth, pp. 53f.
20. Translation by Ward, *The Sayings of the Desert Fathers*.
21. P. Rousseau in Jones, pp. 123f.
22. Louth in Jones, pp. 184f.
23. E. Trueman Dicken in Jones, pp. 366f.
24. Ibid., pp. 368f.
25. F. Zimmermann in Jones, pp. 498f.
26. L. Jacobs in Jones, pp. 491f.
27. Lewis and Slater, *The Study of Religions*, p. 39.
28. Bouquet, *Sacred Books of the World*, pp. 119f.
29. Ibid., pp. 229f.

30. Humphreys, *Buddhism*, pp. 109f.

31. Kumar, *Vision*, pp. 2f.

32. Allchin, *The Kingdom of Love and Knowledge*, p. 184.

33. Allchin, p. 182. There is a biography by Armstrong, *Evelyn Underhill*.

34. There is a biography by Furlong, *Merton*.

35. His autobiography to 1954 is *The Golden String*. For his subsequent eastern turn see the biography by Spink, *A Sense of the Sacred*.

2   Themes of Wisdom and Contemplation

1. For this and the previous paragraph see Eliade (ed.), *Encyclopedia of Religion* 14, pp. 19, 342f.; Guillaume, *Islam*, p. 150.

2. Kumar, *The Vision of Kabir*, p. 96.

3. XXVII after Lin Yutang, *The Wisdom of China*, p. 41. (A different interpretation in Lau p. 84.)

4. Lin Yutang, p. 49.

5. Lin Yutang, p. 246.

6. Schwartz, *The World of Thought in Ancient China*, p. 88.

7. Creel, *Chinese Thought from Confucius to Mao Tse-tung*, p. 75.

8. McGinn (ed.), *Christian Spirituality*, p. 407.

9. Ward, *The Sayings of the Desert Fathers*, p. 62.

10. Ward, p. 4.

11. Winston, *Philo of Alexandria*, pp. 47f. (from *The Contemplative Life*, IV).

12. Parrinder, *Mysticism in the World's Religions*, pp. 31f.

13. Kumar, p. 151.

14. Parrinder, p. 50.

15. *Tao Te Ching* XIX, trs. Waley, *The Way and Its Power*, p. 166.

16. *Tao Te Ching* XXII, after Lin Yutang, pp. 37f.

17. *Tao Te Ching* XLVI, after Lin Yutang, p. 50.

18. *Tao Te Ching* XLVII, after Lin Yutang, p. 50 and Waley p. 199.

19. *Tao Te Ching* LIX, Waley, p. 213.

20. Lin Yutang, p. 245.

21. Underhill, *Practical Mysticism*, pp. 23f.

22. Ibid., p. 27.

23. Louth, *The Origins of the Christian Mystical Tradition*, p. 8.

24. Lin Yutang, p. 249.

25. After Lin Yutang, p. 249.

26. Kumar, p. 48.

27. Von Rad, *Wisdom in Israel*, pp. 24, 30, 50.

28. Waley, pp. 46f.

29. Weil, *Waiting on God*, pp. 66f.

30. Merton, *Seeds of Contemplation*, p. 95.

31. Nouwen, *The Way of the Heart*, p. 76.

32. Williams, *The Wound of Knowledge*, pp. 76f.

33. Underhill, p. 4.

34. Johnston, *The Mirror Mind*, p. 97.
35. Weil, pp. 66–76.
36. Stanwood (ed.), *William Law*, p. 179.
37. Ward, p. 247.
38. Ward, p. 2.
39. Louth, p. 155.
40. Louth, p. 171.
41. Merton, *Seeds*, p. 63.
42. *Tao Te Ching* VIII, after Lin Yutang, p. 30.
43. Ibid., LXVI; Waley, p. 224.
44. Ibid., II; after Lin Yutang, p. 28.
45. Ibid., X; after Lin Yutang, p. 31 (another interpretation in Lau, p. 66).
46. Kumar, p. 136.
47. Von Rad, p. 108.
48. Underhill, pp. 23f.
49. Inge, *Christian Mysticism*, p. 8.
50. Johnston, *The Inner Eye of Love*, p. 20.
51. *Tao Te Ching* LXVII; after Lin Yutang, p. 59.
52. Parrinder, p. 62.
53. Guillaume, p. 151.
54. Parrinder, pp. 131f.
55. Epstein, *Judaism*, pp. 229f.
56. Epstein, p. 242.
57. Epstein, p. 250.
58. Underhill, p. 91.
59. Winston, pp. 141–3.
60. Johnston, *Inner Eye*, pp. 16–18.
61. *Tao Te Ching* I, XIV; after Lin Yutang, pp. 27, 33.
62. Parrinder, p. 72.
63. *Tao Te Ching* LXXI; after Lin Yutang, p. 61.
64. After Lin Yutang, p. 255.
65. Ward, p. 2.
66. Von Rad, p. 293.
67. Von Rad, p. 99.
68. Von Rad, p. 313.
69. Von Rad, p. 318.
70. Buber, *I and Thou*, p. 12.
71. *Kagemni*; see McKane, *Proverbs*, p. 66.
72. *Ani*; after Pritchard, p. 420.
73. Waley, p. 59.
74. Waley, p. 57.
75. *Tao Te Ching* LV; Lin Yutang, p. 54.
76. Schwarz, p. 123.
77. Louth, p. 172.
78. Ward, p. 18.
79. Ward, p. 246.
80. Guillaume, p. 144.

81. Ward, pp. viif.
82. Merton, *Seeds*, p. 87.
83. Rowley, *Submission in Suffering*, p. 37.
84. After Lin Yutang, pp. 100f.
85. After Lin Yutang, p. 102.
86. *Tao Te Ching* VIII; Lin Yutang, p. 30.
87. Lin Yutang, p. 100.
88. Ibid., p. 177.
89. Creel, pp. 107f.
90. Creel, p. 112.
91. Kumar, p. 147.
92. *Ptah-hotep*; see McKane, p. 61.
93. *Ptah-hotep*; Pritchard, p. 414.
94. In the thirteenth of her *Revelations of Divine Love*.
95. After Buber, p. 31.
96. *The Ascent of Mount Carmel* I.1. His complete works are translated by Allison Peers.
97. Cf. Parrinder, p. 58.
98. As note 15.
99. *Tao Te Ching* XLVIII; after Waley, p. 201.
100. After Creel, p. 111.
101. Kumar, p. 175.
102. Cited in Williams, p. 102 from her *Guidelines for Mystical Prayer*, pp. 101–2.
103. Kumar, p. 42.
104. Louth, pp. 57–8.
105. Teresa of Avila, *Foundations* 5:8; Allison Peers, vol. 3, p. 22.
106. Ward, p. 70.
107. Humphreys, p. 114.
108. Mascaro, *Bhagavad Gita*, p. 32.
109. After Mascaro, p. 58.
110. After Mascaro, pp. 62f.
111. Pritchard, pp. 432f.
112. Williams, p. 128.
113. Williams, pp. 134f.
114. Von Rad, p. 318.
115. Louth, pp. 3, 193–4.
116. Louth, p. 39.
117. Louth, pp. 19f.
118. Louth, pp. 62f.
119. Louth, pp. 80–97.
120. Johnston, *Inner Eye*, p. 20.
121. *Scale of Perfection* 2:41; wording as cited by Parrinder, p. 151.
122. *Revelations of Divine Love* I.5; cited by Parrinder, p. 151.
123. Merton, *Seeds*, p. 80.
124. Merton, *The New Man*, pp. 15–17.
125. Stanza 1 of his poem 'Wonder'; cited by Parrinder, p. 157.
126. *Tao Te Ching* IV; Lin Yutang, p. 29.

127. *Tao Te Ching* XXXIV; Lin Yutang, p. 44.
128. Schwarz, p. 189.
129. Humphreys, p. 117.
130. *Gita* 18.20, 52–56; after Mascaro, pp. 116, 119–20.
131. Kumar, p. 177.
132. From the text set by R. Vaughan Williams in his inspiring *Sea Symphony*: IV. The Explorers.
133. Inge, pp. 3–4, 41.
134. Inge, p. 41.
135. *The Scale of Perfection* 2:21.
136. Merton, *The New Man*, p. 15.
137. *My Job*, pp. 29, 66.
138. 'He fixed (the heart) to her' – a dative suffix.
139. Ward, p. 8.
140. Ward, p. 104.
141. Von Rad, p. 69.
142. Underhill, p. 3.
143. Cited and discussed by Davies, *The Theology of William Blake*, p. 80.
144. *Republic* VII.517, referred to by Louth, p. 3.

3   *Wisdom and Contemplation in the Psalms*

1. There is a good reproduction in Michalowski, *The Art of Ancient Egypt*, no. 494.
2. Eliade, 14, p. 342; 13, pp. 30–1.
3. My *The Psalms Come Alive*, pp. 72–101.
4. B. Duhm, *Die Psalmen*, pp. 427f.; my translation here.
5. J. Neale, *Commentary on the Psalms* IV, p. 3.
6. Eliade, 14, p. 342.
7. Taylor, *The Way of Heaven*, p. 24.
8. 'I shall make thee love writing more than thy own mother' – Pritchard, p. 432; cf. McKane, p. 86.
9. After Pritchard, p. 415.
10. Smullyan, *The Tao is Silent*, p. 3.
11. Péguy, *The Mystery of the Holy Innocents*, pp. 76–8.
12. Eliade, 14, p. 342.
13. Kumar, p. 85.
14. *Merikare*; Pritchard, p. 415.
15. *Merikare*; see McKane, p. 74.
16. My *Kingship and the Psalms*, pp. 143f.
17. For a comprehensive survey and discussion see my *Kingship and the Psalms*.
18. Gardiner, *Ancient Egyptian Onomastica*.
19. Pritchard, pp. 369f.

4   *Wisdom Calls to the Modern World*

1. *The Marriage of East and West*, p. 28.
2. *Return to the Centre*, p. 68.
3. *Marriage*, p. 41.
4. Egan, *What Are They Saying About Mysticism?*, pp. 11f., referring to the work of Richard Bucke.
5. *Marriage*, pp. 22f.
6. In Eliade, 1, p. 507.
7. *Marriage*, p. 43.
8. *Return*, p. 18.
9. *Return*, p. 47.
10. *Return*, p. 62.
11. Recent treatments of the Song include commentaries by R. Gordis, M. Pope, R. Davidson; see also Falk, *Love Lyrics from the Bible*, and Goulder, *The Song of Fourteen Songs*.
12. *Return*, p. 118.
13. *Return*, p. 106.

List of Works Cited

Allchin, A. M., *The Kingdom of Love and Knowledge*, 1979
Anderson, G. W., (ed.), *Tradition and Interpretation*, 1979
Armstrong, C. J. R., *Evelyn Underhill 1875–1941*, 1975
Bergant, Dianne, *What Are They Saying About Wisdom Literature?*, 1984
Bouquet, A. C., *Sacred Books of the World*, 1954
Buber, Martin, *I and Thou*, trs. R. G. White, 1937
Creel, H. G., *Chinese Thought from Confucius to Mao Tse-tung*, 1954
Crenshaw, J. L., *Old Testament Wisdom: An Introduction*, 1981
Danby, H., *The Mishnah, Translated*, 1933
Davidson, Robert, *Ecclesiastes and the Song of Solomon*, Daily Study
    Bible, 1986
Davies, J. G., *The Theology of William Blake*, 1948
Duhm, B., *Die Psalmen*, ed. K. Marti, 1899, 1922
Eaton, J. H., *Kingship and the Psalms*, 1975, revised ed. 1986
— , *The Psalms Come Alive*, 1984, 1986
— , *Job*, Old Testament Guides, 1985
Egan, H. D., *What Are They Saying about Mysticism?*, 1982
Eliade, Mircéa (ed.), *The Encyclopedia of Religion*, 1987
Epstein, Isidore, *Judaism*, 1959
Falk, Marcia, *Love Lyrics from the Bible: A Translation and Literary Study
    of the Song of Songs*, 1982
Furlong, Monica, *Merton, A Biography*, 1980, 1982
Gardiner, A. H., *Ancient Egyptian Onomastica*, 1947
Gordis, Robert, *The Song of Songs and Lamentations*, revised ed. 1974
Goulder, M. D., *The Song of Fourteen Songs*. 1986
Griffiths, Bede, *The Golden String: An Autobiography*, 1954, 1964
— , *Return to the Centre*, 1976
— , *The Marriage of East and West*, 1982
Guillaume, A., *Islam*, 1954
Helck, W. (ed.), *Lexikon der Ägyptologie 3*, 1980
Herford, R. Travers, *The Ethics of the Talmud: Sayings of the Fathers*,
    1925, 1962
Hilton, Walter, *The Scale of Perfection*, modernized by an oblate of
    Solesmes, 1927
Humphreys, Christmas, *Buddhism*, 1951

Inge, W. R., *Christian Mysticism*, 1899, 1933

Johnston, William, *The Inner Eye of Love*, 1978

— , *The Mirror Mind*, 1981

Jones, C., Wainwright, G., Yarnold, E. (eds.), *The Study of Spirituality*, 1986

Julian of Norwich, *Revelations of Divine Love*, ed. Grace Warrack, 1901f.

Kumar, Sehdev, *The Vision of Kabir: Love Poems of a Fifteenth Century Weaver and Sage*, 1984

Lau, D. C., *Lao Tzu: Tao Te Ching*, 1963

Lewis, H. D., and Slater, R. L., *The Study of Religions*, 1969

Yutang, Lin, *The Wisdom of China*, 1944

Louth, A., *The Origins of the Christian Mystical Tradition, From Plato to Denys*, 1981

McGinn, B., and Meyendorff, J. (eds.), *Christian Spirituality: Origins to the Twelfth Century*, I, II, 1985, 1986

McKane, William, *Proverbs: A New Approach*, 1970

Mascaro, Juan (trs.), *The Bhagavad Gita*, 1962

Merton, Thomas, *Seeds of Contemplation*, 1950

— , *The New Man*, 1963

Michalowski, K., *The Art of Ancient Egypt*, 1969

Neale, J. M. and Littledale, R. F., *A Commentary on the Psalms from Primitive and Mediaeval Writers*, revised ed. 1883

Nouwen, Henri, *The Way of the Heart*, 1981

Parrinder, G., *Mysticism in the World's Religions*, 1976

Peers, E. Allison (trs.), *St John of the Cross: Complete Works*, 1947

— , *St Teresa of Avila: Complete Works*, 1946

Péguy, Charles, *The Mystery of the Holy Innocents and Other Poems*, trs. Pansy Pakenham, 1956

Pope, Marvin H., *The Song of Songs*, Anchor Bible, 1977

Rad, G. von, *Wisdom in Israel* (German 1970), 1972

Rowley, H. H., *Submission in Suffering and Other Essays on Eastern Thought*, 1951

Schwartz, B. I., *The World of Thought in Ancient China*, 1985

Smullyan, Raymond M., *The Tao is Silent*, 1977

Spink, Kathryn, *A Sense of the Sacred: A Biography of Bede Griffiths*, 1988

Stanwood, P. G. (ed.), *William Law: A Serious Call, etc.*, 1978

Taylor, Rodney, *The Way of Heaven: Introduction to the Confucian Way of Life*, Iconography of Religions, 1986

Underhill, Evelyn, *Practical Mysticism*, 1914

Waley, A., *The Way and Its Power*, 1934

Ward, Benedicta, *The Sayings of the Desert Fathers*, 1981

Weil, Simone, *Waiting on God*, 1959

Williams, Rowan, *The Wound of Knowledge*, 1979

Winston, David (trs.), *Philo of Alexandria: The Contemplative Life etc.*, 1981